Crush Your Leadership Paradigm:

The Case for Leadership Coaching

Dr. Phil Millage

ISBN -10:1546605193

ISBN-13: 978-1546605195

Acknowledgments

First, I want to thank all those who have participated in my professional development, including the hundreds of managerial people and CEOs whose wisdom has informed my thinking. Sometimes their influence has extended over a period of years. Occasionally their impact is instantaneous. For example, I once heard a commencement speaker (a successful businessman) note the importance of learning that his most important decision was his second decision—to fix the first decision. What a simple but useful insight.

By providing me with concrete guiding principles, my father helped me to form the moral foundation of my life. Armed with only an eighth-grade education, he took life as it came. When Dad was growing up, an eighth-grade education was commonplace. Fortunately for me, my father possessed a lion's share of "common sense." He often said, "Common sense should be uncommon sense because it isn't that common." I benefited from watching him put his common sense into action and become successful.

I was blessed to have tremendous teachers, one of whom taught me that teaching was "not a right but rather a privilege." Dr. Hamilton also said, "Aren't we lucky to work in the greatest profession?" Show me a CEO who doesn't realize that the job includes teaching, modeling behavior, and ultimately creating a culture, and I will show you a person in serious need of a coach.

I also want to acknowledge my family, especially my wife. She has demonstrated an attitude of unconditional acceptance. Long-term relationships help us find the keys to what is important in life. My children learned the value of patience having me as their father, and I learned patience by being their father.

I love each of my children equally, and each has their unique talents and strengths. My older son is very much like his father. As you can imagine, this is both good news and bad news. Those whom we are "like" tend to challenge us the most. Therefore Josh has been the child who has been willing to put his father to the test intellectually. Thankfully he has successfully challenged some of my most dearly held (yet unwisely conceived) presuppositions. More often than not, his view has been correct. In this book, I argue for healthy conflict, that is, conflict defined by differences of opinion yet tempered by a consideration of others. Josh and I practice this in life.

My daughter has demonstrated the value of inner strength. She is a people person, and thus has many friends, but she accepts challenges that will allow her "strong will" to be put to work for worthy causes. It is impressive to watch. My younger son demonstrates unconditional love and true loyalty to his friends. His loyalty gets tested and he hangs on to his people. Jacob is slow to distance himself from people who fail. Loyalty is compelling to those who are watching—and in business it positively impacts a corporate culture.

Great leaders learn both positive and negative principles from those they are the closest to. A good rule is to apply the positive principles and try not to repeat the negative ones. Look for the good and you will see talent at work in the lives of others.

CONTENTS

Chapter 1

Introductions

The ongoing theme of this book is to work your strengths and crush your leadership paradigm. Breaking your old paradigm allows the "real you" to emerge and your personal productivity to improve. Once you know yourself, you will be positioned to accomplish much more with your life. The goal is to refocus your energy so you can exploit your talents and strengths.

The only human being you need to fully understand is yourself! Once you have an excellent picture of yourself, seeing the value in others becomes less challenging. Learning about the "real you" often requires a lifetime. The goal of this book is to demonstrate how you can speed up the process.

Once we are clear about our own talents and strengths, we can begin to appreciate the differences in others. Learning to use our own talent frees us to outsource tasks to people with complementary strengths. Business processes can also be tailored to better serve the CEO.

Fortunately people are not machines. C. S. Lewis rightly said, "There are no ordinary people." We start our journey with the assumption that everyone has tremendous talent. And you, as a keen executive, can benefit by tapping your own potential and subsequently helping others see—and build success on—their talent.

This book was written specifically for CEOs and other top executives. It is also an excellent resource for anyone aspiring to hold a top leadership position. The text alone serves as a coaching tool, but an underlying understanding is that a CEO who seriously wants to maximize personal and corporate potential needs to hire an executive coach. Collaboration with a coach provides a CEO with a forum for addressing challenging questions. In the coaching relationship, the first step is for the coach to help the CEO discover and fully employ his or her strengths. When this process is successful, it provides the foundation for a positive shift in performance. The goal is to help the CEO achieve a personal and professional "paradigm shift."

Writing this book, I realize there is a personal connection between author and reader, just as there is, or should be, in the coaching process. So let me introduce myself by relating highlights (and lowlights) of my professional journey. As you read, why not reflect about times in your life where you had a bad fit and a good fit. Imagine if over the years you were privileged to have a coach to assist you with your professional development, what a difference it could make in your career and in your current organization.

First Job: Bad Fit

As a young man, my first job was at Prudential Insurance Company at the North Central Home Office in Minneapolis. My undergraduate degree wasn't in business but in social studies. I took a job in the marketing department, where most of my work was simply shuffling paper. I would take information from one report and convert it into a format more palatable for my vice president to digest.

Luckily a small part of my job involved fieldwork evaluation of sales people in Michigan, and I truly enjoyed working with salespeople. Unfortunately that engaging portion of the job represented only about 10 percent of my responsibilities. I lasted about a year and a half on the job, and overall it was a very painful experience. I'm sure my wife could testify about how wonderful it is to be married to someone who is unhappy at work. She was living 650 miles from home and newly married to an unhappy guy. I'm sorry that this sounds a bit like reality television.

Prudential was and continues to be a very good company with flexible working hours, excellent benefits, and many fine people. My problem wasn't the organization or its employees. It was working in a position where I spent 90 percent of my time in activities that did not engage my talents. Additionally, I was young and not well equipped to deal with the emotions I was experiencing. I was not trained for business, and I took a corporate position merely to put food on the table.

Prudential's policy was to hire young people with liberal arts backgrounds and try to fit them in. I think most of what Prudential did in this regard was very good for young people looking for opportunity and an organization that was willing to train and mentor them. I recall being convinced that my parents had raised a young man who was facing fifty years of work—work that he would certainly not enjoy.

I compensated for my unhappiness at Prudential by developing a clock-watcher attitude. Incidentally, when you watch a clock face—the clock hands don't move. We had flexible hours, so I would arrive early (7 a.m.), which freed me to leave early at 3:00 p.m., actually at about 2:55. I would find an excuse to leave my little cubicle five or ten minutes early. I would decide to use the restroom or talk to a colleague at a different location, whatever could get me close to the exit. I would rush to my car so I could hit the Interstate before the afternoon rush hour.

The side effects were evident. I sucked it up at work. I imagine I looked very much like an average new hire at Prudential. I was hoping the job would buy me some time to think things through and look for options. I experienced a great deal of stress. I was not prepared for office politics, the egos of the people above me, and the subtle conflict that rides under the surface with coworkers. As you can imagine, I was ready to see a psychologist.

At Prudential, it should have occurred to me that I was "a duck out of the water." During this painful episode, the human resources staff never interviewed me to see how things were going. I'm guessing "workplace engagement" wasn't even taught in college during that time, and it certainly was not part of the corporate communication or accountability system. I am still very grateful for the opportunity Prudential provided me. Since work engagement has become a mantra for corporate America, things are much better today.

I had nothing to compare this experience to. My inability to reflect and evaluate my situation made me miss an important fact that could have helped clarify everything. Finding a job that used my talents could have made a huge difference. I would have hit my stride in my career had I known about talent and strengths.

Finding My Stride

Thankfully I enjoyed a contrasting experience when I took a part-time sales job for Sears. I sold lawn tractors, chainsaws, fencing, and so on. Early in the job experience, my Sears supervisor excitedly announced, "Phil, you are the top part-time salesman in the Twin Cities area." How could I be so amazing at one job and such a pathetic loser at the other one? The only thing that can consistently explain notable successful professional experiences is engagement.

If I had carefully reflected about previous successes and failures, in educational and leadership settings, my talents would have been easily recognizable. I am a people person. I'm actually sort of the crazy entertainer type. Some would describe my personality as "off the leash." My off-beat people orientation worked like a charm in sales, especially in the nontechnical aisles.

So what does an unhappy college boy do? He goes back to school for an MBA. My graduate program gave me a very broad business learning experience, and I loved it. The variety of required courses along with some consulting in the community, working for professors, meeting colleagues who worked in different industries, class conversations, and so on—all helped to inform my thinking. These combined experiences gave me a global perspective and significantly provided an opportunity to try out several strategic options. In short, I fell in love with marketing, the world of ideas, and the joy of collaborative teamwork. The rest is history.

When I finished the MBA, I was hired by a small university to teach a cross-section of courses that fit my talents well. During my teaching career, at four universities, I eventually acquired a doctorate and taught more than fifty-four different college preparations. What a learning experience.

There is some truth to the adage, "You never know a subject until you teach it." Teaching was a wonderful education for me. The variety of courses I taught seemed to fit me perfectly. My primary strength is "ideation," and the classroom was a place to try out ideas. Universities, though bureaucratic and rule oriented, typically let people teach in whatever way their creativity directs.

Oddly enough, my identified talent for ideation describes why my sense of humor works. I make easy connections to unrelated situations that provide fodder for humor. A person whose mind is moving quickly over random ideas sees the connections of humor. In my case, by seeing the ridiculous things I do and then understanding how it happened helps others relate to stupid things they have done.

As an example, I accidentally went into to a McDonald's restroom in Gatlinburg, Tennessee. I sat down and became very emotionally upset when I heard female voices. As I quickly exited the restroom, a couple of older ladies looked absolutely horrified. As I stepped out into a full dining room, a man (apparently closely related to the late comedian Don Rickles) said in a loud voice, "Hey buddy, did you notice anything different about that restroom?" Now everyone in the restaurant is staring at me (and yes, Judy and I were with friends). A couple of women seated at a table about twelve feet away were pointing in my direction, and their jaws seemed to moving in a somewhat angry fashion. After a few minutes everything quieted down until a young teenage girl came over to my table and said, "Sir, you left your books in our bathroom."

One other example involves simply perceiving humorous connections in life. When the movie *Dumb and Dumber* had been out for a few months, the dollar theater in Carmel, Indiana, had a large sign that said, "This theater is currently under new management," and about one foot under that was the movie sign: "Currently showing: *Dumb and Dumber*." I almost drove off the road laughing. Ideation talent is all about seeing and building connections involving unrelated information.

When teaching, my "ideation" strength allowed me to follow my heart in each course. Left to my true talents and strengths, I ended up enjoying it all. I built new ideas into every course, and I found connections to other disciplines. I was able to give each course a unique creative spin. The spark I provided came directly out of my strengths. I never carefully followed the textbook but used it as a database in each course. I constantly searched for connections to real business and to innovative ideas. I love people and seeing them advance, so what was not to love about the job (well, there was the bureaucracy).

Each course focused on creative projects developed by student teams. I played the role of the consultant by being both the devil's advocate and by infusing new ideas into the process. In my third year of teaching, I was named "professor of the year" for the entire university. When you teach and fully employ your strengths, it is called "working in the flow." I thrived. Teaching was less about me, and more about the power of student engagement. Both then and now, I summarize my mission as "I am an idea person who is a true advocate for both individuals and organizations."

Early in my tenure as professor, I was lured away from the university by two of my talented students, asking me to work in the family building company. They hired me in my area of expertise, marketing. This little company operated out of a living room in a small Indiana town that still only has fewer than a thousand residents. The interview was, well, interesting. At the beginning, the owner said, "I don't know what questions to ask you, so I'd like you to both ask and then answer your own questions." As you can imagine, I threw myself softball questions and got the job.

To demonstrate how naïve I was . . . I asked my future boss a question that merited a follow-up. "Do we have health insurance?" Answer, "Yes!" I should have then asked, "Who pays for it?" I was also remiss in not asking another question, "Do I have a marketing budget?" The answer would have been "You are the budget, Phil."

Good news. When I got to the job, my boss's advice was "Just do your own thing and make us some money." I was green, so I just followed my heart and my talents. What else could I do, having no marketing budget? So we (the sons and I) cold-called nearly every business within a sixty-mile radius of Indianapolis. I wrote articles for various local papers and industry-specific publications. I created my own ads; one got some national recognition. I discovered that I had some copywriting ability. I spoke to every local service organization, community development group, Chamber of Commerce, or business that would let me in the door. Basically I hit every place that would let me speak. This type of professional speaking is lovingly referred to as "the rubber-chicken circuit," that is, the circuit lets a person speak to a wide range of service and community organizations. The compensation, if any, is negligible—a free chicken dinner—but it is a good way to promote one's self or to make connections for the business one represents.

We used *Guerrilla Marketing* tactics from Jay Conrad Levinson's first edition. That book sparked many wonderful marketing ideas and some creative ideation of my own. By the end of three years, we were the thirteenth-largest builder and seventh-largest developer in metropolitan Indianapolis. I had an absolute blast in that job. It is amazing what can result when you give people the freedom to work hard based on their talents. It is interesting to note that even one's selection of books to read is largely driven by one's talents.

Teaching provides a natural segue to what is lovingly referred to as the "real world." For example, I've asked many of my past colleagues why they enjoyed research, or why the desired a deeper knowledge in some subject area. The most common answer was "out of curiosity." This is true for me and explains why I began to fall in love with the real world of business. As I moved from talent to strength, I intrinsically knew my talent could be and should be put to work in something more than a theoretical exercise such as teaching. On that journey, a strength emerges.

I was a business professor who hadn't experienced much "real business." Since my temperament oriented me toward people combined with my love of ideas, I had a deep desire to put my ideas to work in a business. Consulting was the easiest first step, because it was low risk (I was just advising), and whatever job I took, I could explore new ideas at the library and gain practical knowledge by talking to successful people. I found that a typical business leader did not have the time to do the research that was needed to move his or her organization forward. Thus, even though I lacked practical experience, I was bringing new ideas, and I was not limited by being a captive of the organization (a captive to their paradigm). I didn't have to worry as much about supporting existing methods or closely supporting those who were currently running the organization. All I had to do was create ideas that worked.

My ideation talent was a good fit; I was talented at finding new approaches. Additionally, I could harvest the best ideas from the leaders in the current industry. Finally, the ideas that were working well in unrelated industries could be applied in my client's industry. My "ideation" talent was fast becoming my "ideation" strength. I fell in love with helping others succeed and enjoyed seeing people grow in their careers. My talents were further developed into strengths as I consulted in more than one hundred companies and served on a variety or boards and in community organizations.

Many of the people I coach are developing their talents, but they are not fully engaged. A CEO who is only 50 to 60 percent instead of 80 to 90 percent engaged is forgoing an enormous amount of bottom-line success. Once a CEO is fully engaged, we can work building that talent into a legitimate strength.

As noted, I give some credit for my speaking and teaching success to my sense of humor, another personal strength. I've also learned to work with my impatient streak. I like to move through work quickly. I'm always trying to move the nickel or close the sale or start the new process. One of my favorite lines is "If you don't know what to do, at least, move your body!" I just want to get things moving.

When analyzing my consulting/coaching work with more than 120 companies, I realize that I am generally hired for my ideas. Much of this could have been recognized early in my career had I taken more input from mentors and coaches or simply taken a strengths assessment. I was doing business, but did not know how to label it. Likewise as a marketing professor, I heard many adult students say, "I've been doing marketing my entire life, I just didn't know it was called marketing."

Over the span of my career, coaching, particularly in the field of marketing, grew to become the primary focus. My primary focus was marketing and nearly every marketing consult started by my needing to move people to positions in which they were most effective. Why spend money on "promotion" when you can secure great results by simply getting people in the right positions? For example, if a person is dominant and pushy, it might not work well to have that person serving in customer service. I found myself spending more and more time analyzing people. Because I had a natural love of people, I was moving them to positions that fit them better and made them more productive. In other words, I was working to get people engaged even before I knew what it was called.

As a coach you begin with a firm's business issues, but then it immediately gets personal. A CEO might say, "Help me understand why my VP seems to be so unmotivated." In reality, the need for engagement is hard to miss. The need for engagement just seems to emerge. Most businesses fail to truly apply talent in a specific way. In other words, what one lacks in talent can often be transferred to a different employee who can do it well.

Identifying One's Natural Talents

When working as an executive coach, one of the first things I suggest, even require, is for the executive to take the Clifton StrengthsFinder assessment, the gold standard for determining one's natural talents, which, when developed, become strengths. The website where it can be inexpensively purchased, www.gallupstrengthscenter.com, boasts of the test's use by more than 15 million people. A good amount of helpful information comes with the assessment report. The

Gallup website also provides access to excellent Gallup publications and assessments. It is the best way to start your growth journey. Time and again I've seen executives, and eventually their staff, benefit from using the StrengthsFinder tool. It assesses thirty-four talent areas. One's top-five talents should be affirmed, valued, and developed in ways that bolster a company's success. For an extra fee, one can see one's personal ranking of all thirty-four talents.

The top five talents reflect the real you. Six through ten are important in a supportive role; over time some might rise in rank, and some talents in the top five might move down. A problem can occur when one decides that low-ranking talents need remedial work. The lower-ranked talents will not be the ones that lead you to success. One caveat: If a talent produces negative attitudes or consequences, try to minimize it, but don't spend a lifetime trying to make it into a strength. For example, I am not particularly focused; focus ranks low for me. So occasionally when pushed to provide a quick response, I might respond by, "I'm tired of hearing about focus when we haven't adequately explored the options." I might say it more forcefully than that. I've had to work on that by letting the "focus people" begin to sharpen my expansive list of ideas.

As an example, and to further my goal of connecting to you as a reader, I include a summary of my top-five talents, as assessed by the Clifton StrengthsFinder.

1. **Ideation.** (I'm 100 percent an idea person.) You would think universities would be the best place for trying out

new ideas, but in that milieu ideas are not appreciated unless based on research. Unfortunately 90 percent of research is based on what has happened in the past and not focused toward the future. "Blue Ocean" break-through ideation (based on the book *Blue Ocean Strategy,* by W. Chan Kim and Renée Mauborgne) is not what most universities are about. For example, the process of accreditation is about keeping to standards, not about breaking the rules. On the other hand, a business must break the rules and creatively destroy/crush old paradigms if it is to profit long-term. Profit is simply a dividend to be used for future development.

2. **Activator.** (I'm always pushing to get going on change.) I despise inertia. Imagine the problem this causes in higher education. Universities are much like the government: leadership by committees. Contrast this with the business world: the more bureaucracy, the less nimble the business. An executive coach who focuses on growth would never want to coach for a CEO whose goal is to maintain the status quo. Playing defense is indefensible in business. If a high-school basketball team that plays Indiana University gets IU to agree only to play defense, eventually the high school players will make a shot and win.

3. **Connectedness.** (I possess a broad view of the world, and I see how all the divergent parts of the world are connected. This has allowed me to consistently maintain a global corporate perspective.) Again I refer to the academic milieu: universities tend to operate in silos; the

biology people rarely see or speak to the art people . . . You get the idea. I've seen this in business, but not in growing and expanding businesses.

4. **Command.** (I believe "now" is the time to make decisions.) I have consulted for a few large universities. The conventional university strategy is to fly in the experts and duplicate the best-in-class processes successfully employed at a different institution. This often happens in business, but the sharpest CEOs are typically cutting a new path rather than duplicating something that is working well.

5. **Responsibility.** (I believe we should behave like adults and honor our commitments.) I am very serious about people, myself and others, needing to take responsibility. I love working through strategic planning, working on a corporate turn-around project, and creative problem solving. I enjoy helping to make dysfunctional organizations change and turn toward functionality.

Is StrengthsFinder the central point of coaching? No, but it is an excellent point of entry, and it is a helpful guide along the way as you work to build talents into strengths. Talents that aren't developed into strengths can have negative consequences, including fomenting problems with turnover; failed initiatives; dysfunctional teams; unfair treatment of low-performing employees; and occasionally employee retaliation against the organization, such as theft of intellectual property.

This Book—and More

Upon reading this short book, a CEO will be stimulated to consider the value of employing a coach. This is not an exhaustive encyclopedia of coaching, but it will provide insight into how to hire and use a coach for the purpose of professional growth and ultimately to enhance organizational success.

Strength-focused professional growth is challenging without the input of a professional who has the education, experience, and commitment to help the CEO advance. A coach will be a CEO's greatest advocate. In a 2013 Executive Coaching Survey, undertaken by the Miles Group in concert with the Stanford Graduate School of Business, David F. Larcker noted "nearly 100%" of the surveyed CEOs indicated that they enjoyed the leadership coaching process.

Much like the Miles Group study, this book advances the idea that a coach can help achieve a superior return on investment. Additionally, CEOs will understand why so many CEOs haven't used a coach—the stigma often associated with hiring a coach. Finally, the book will provide the crucial information enabling CEOs to move forward in their search for an executive coach.

For the younger person who might not be able to afford an executive coach, I recommend that you take a Clifton StrengthsFinder to learn about your talent. Focus on your top five talents while developing the supportive talents ranked as six through ten. Truly spend time working on fully understanding this powerful tool.

Once you finished taking the StrengthsFinder assessment, I recommend you find a mentor who can help you build your talents into strengths. Much like a CEO, your goal is to master a few key areas based on your talents. Remember, the role of a great mentor is to provide input that will help you grow as a leader.

Then list your top values and use your top five talents to create a branding statement that describes you and can be used to create a thirty-second presentation needed to describe your talents and how you will advance the organization. A sample branding statement for me? "I will use my ideation strength to help you crush your current paradigm. Ultimately my goal is to become a trusted advocate for both you and your organization."

But you're not convinced that you need a coach— any help beyond what's available on the StrengthsFinder site? Keep reading. You just might change your mind.

Chapter 2

A Coach? Convince Me

What can a coach do for you? Great question. In short, here's my answer: The best use of an executive coach is

1. To help the CEO become more effective and efficient
2. To help everyone more fully use their talents and strengths (starting with the top management team)
3. To help motivate the entire organization (corporate culture is critical)
4. To help the organization grow
5. To work with struggling top executives (never the focus; it should come only as you interact during 1 and 2 above)

We'll first focus on category 1—how coaching can bring out the best in you, personally and professionally.

The Coach's Role

But before we get there, let's address more basic questions: What is the role of a coach? Is a coach really needed? I believe by the time your finish this book, you will agree that every top executive needs a coach. One of my past clients (very successful) said, "Every leader needs a shrink." Not that a coach is a shrink; nor is a coach a friend who takes on an informal mentoring role. As important as mentors can be, they may be too close (personally) to "speak truth to power." A coach should not be hired as a result of a prior close personal connection to either the CEO or others in the firm. The right coach will have the experience, education, credibility, and autonomy needed to help the CEO grow as a leader. The coach is somewhat like a temporary employee with whom the CEO feels comfortable sharing confidences. Often the relationship becomes one of coproduction of better ideas, better processes, finding ways to enhance productivity, and certainly clarifying the best ways the CEO can employ her or his talents/strengths.

The coach should not be seeking a permanent position. This means that the coach doesn't (and should not) have line decision-making authority. Coaches don't hire, fire, and rarely do they make decisions that involve the use of significant resources, except as related to their individual contractual obligations. Coaches are not captives of the organization, and they work directly for the CEO. A coach must challenge the CEO, but the CEO is required to call the shots. Understanding where coaching influence ends and CEO decision-making begins is critical. The coach is not a decision maker for the firm. A coach's job is to make the CEO effective and efficient. If successful, the entire organization will benefit.

I once worked with a medium-sized firm led by a chairman whose son was the CEO. After building a strategic marketing program that delivered substantial financial results, we were positioned to go public. The son wanted to hire me as the executive vice president; the father wanted me to remain as the key consultant and coach. The father's argument was "Phil will tell us when we are wrong. An executive vice president is more likely to play the political game." The father prevailed.

Do you really think that a subordinate wants to tell the CEO to stay out of things he has no talent for? Not so much. As an interesting example, some CEOs feel they have visual design talent when they do not (neither do I). So they preempt this task and attempt to do it themselves, presumably so they can take the credit for the design work. Think about this: How can a subordinate tell the CEO she should stick to the financials or whatever her talent allows for? Art is not her forte. Why not let an executive coach provide input that might be well received, in concert with pointing out where the CEO has talent that could be more effectively used?

Second example: A CEO hired an expensive but incredibly talented Chicago-based agency to rebrand his firm. After bypassing his marketing people (apparently he felt they weren't good enough), he spent significant financial resources and time to work through what I viewed as an excellent branding process. But ultimately he was unwilling to make the changes recommended by the firm.

Subsequently, he opened the graphic design work and process to novices (with limited design experience), again signaling that he did not value the professional designers in his marketing department. Sadly, though his educational background was in communications, he was failing in that regard. What staff person would be able to tell a CEO that his leadership in the branding effort was ineffectual, to put it mildly? Such an employee might be reassigned to some outpost in Siberia. Being the CEO doesn't make someone an expert at everything.

The coach is in a stronger position to influence a CEO provided the coach is not a captive of the organization. In this situation, an executive coach could have taught an open-minded CEO how to maximize his own talents as well as those of his design staff. In other words, a coach could show the CEO how his formal education in communication would be enhanced by his true talents. Interestingly, the CEO may not even be naturally talented in communication. The coach wants the focus to be on proven talent. The coach would teach the CEO how to make use of talents and strengths currently available in the organization. Also, the coach would help the CEO decide what work might be better outsourced. Finally, the coach would possibly even help the CEO determine how to best communicate to employees why outside help is needed.

Third example: I worked for a large national company that provided group homes and support systems for developmentally disabled adults. The CEO had been promoted because she was a very caring person who had worked her way up through the ranks. When looking at the Gallup information, it was obvious that her talents fell primarily in the Relationship Building themes and in the Strategic Thinking themes. She was absent of any Executing themes and Influencing themes. Therefore, she wasn't talented at "making things happen," and her ideas were not delivered in a persuasive manner. Once she learned the value of leaning on other leaders who were good at executing (making things happen) and influencing (communicating), good results began to happen.

But What about Perception?

Is trial and error a good option? There is a story where the professor asked the student, would you care for some input, or do you prefer the experimental mode of learning? The coach is there to provide input. Exploration can cause major problems when a CEO is not doing what she or he has the talent to perform. Stepping on land mines can help you learn, but you might lose a leg in the process.

Is a coach perceived as a plus or a minus? Some CEOs impose a stigma on the coach-hiring process, fearing the presence of a coach will create a perception of the CEO's psychological deficiency. Still others view having a coach as a sign of prestige. It might even send a somewhat subliminal message to colleagues that the leader is being honed for a new, more significant position. Not hiring a coach because it may be viewed as a deficiency or hiring a coach simply to make one's self "look good" are both ill advised.

How the coach is introduced to the organization is important. I think the best way to introduce a coach is to say, "The coach is tasked with helping to grow the entire organization professionally ultimately with helping our profitability improve." The introduction is worth thinking about before you do it.

But privately CEOs overwhelming agree that they would value some personal advice. What the CEO says about a potential coach can be revealing. CEOs often feel they don't have time to even think about hiring a coach. This statement is living proof that a coach is needed. In life, we make time for what is important! Alternatively, a CEO might say, "We have everyone in the perfect position." So how would this CEO answer a question about engagement? In my opinion, any CEO who is unwilling to address misapplied talent is by that very act signaling the need for a coach. Whom will the CEO listen to? If the CEO lacks the maturity to take professional input from a coach (who promises confidentiality), one has to wonder, whom would that CEO listen to? Certainly, reading is a good method to advance professionally if the acquired knowledge is actually implemented. Still, can one downplay the value of collaboration? All a CEO need say is, "I want another set of eyes." Such a comment expresses confidence, not fear.

CEO burnout is a common problem. It might be said that a CEO who isn't burned out is lying or represents a rare exception to the rule. Few things will reduce stress more than working with a coach who can help with engagement. It would be wise for the CEO to push responsibilities to colleagues who have the appropriate talent or to outsource what the CEO does not have the talent to do well. Retooling based on talent is what is needed.

When a CEO is hesitant about employing a coach, a corporate board may pressure human resource personnel to do so. In this case, the CEO's performance might be driving this push. The board wants the CEO to be successful. A

CEO's success will impact stock values and profitability or nonprofit donor relations. If the CEO fails at the job, the board is likely to make a change. If the CEO is successful, the board is successful. The destinies of the board and the CEO are intertwined. A mandated coaching relationship doesn't always launch well, why not reach out on your own terms?

If a CEO is struggling with the decision to hire a coach, it may be advantageous to schedule an initial meeting off-site. If possible, the CEO should make the final hiring decision, setting a foundation for an affirmative coaching engagement. Both the CEO and coach need to sense the possibility of successful engagement. Few CEOs want a board or human resources department to choose a coach for them.

Is the "coach" label the problem? If the word *coach* becomes the problem, I recommend the CEO find a suitable word to explain the professional he or she is working with. I've been called an "assistant to the president," "personnel development officer," "corporate communication expert." Don't let a concern about a label such as the word *coach* derail the plan for the coaching process.

Secure the Best Coach

An executive coach and CEO should be able to determine in their preliminary meetings whether they have the "chemistry" to work together. Chemistry involves getting along well personally, but it doesn't predict an absence of reasonable conflict. Chemistry can't be taught. It is a little like speed dating; either it works or it doesn't. As you try to articulate characteristics of a coach who would be the best collaborator with you, consider whether this person is a good fit for both you and your organization.

Be specific about both the coach's role and the CEO's responsibilities in reference to the engagement. Good personal chemistry coupled with excellent input can lead to significant plans for success. Often CEOs gain confidence in their coaches. Confidence building is an important goal. Just be careful not to let the CEO start delegating line responsibilities to the coach.

The coaching-client relationship starts casually; then trust is developed, and one hopes this leads to mutually beneficial results.

Authenticity (for both the coach and the CEO) is essential if the coaching process is to be a success. A worthy coach will work only with executives who want to advance themselves personally, professionally and corporately. A coach must not be "window dressing" for an executive, to fool others—a board of directors, a chairman, or employees—into believing the CEO is trying to improve performance.

A CEO's self-knowledge coefficient will be improved greatly by the coaching process. Just initiating the process requires the CEO to be transparent and open. It takes courage for a CEO to take the first step by saying something like:

- I admit I don't know everything required to run my company.
- I'm not a good motivator.
- I see the need for another set of eyes to help me grow as a leader.

Such comments indicate the CEO is "owning" how others view him. As noted earlier, the vast majority of CEOs agree that they would benefit by employing a coach. It won't happen unless the CEO takes the first step.

In 1956 Benjamin Blum and his colleagues, in *The Taxonomy of Educational Objectives*, laid out a taxonomy that classifies levels of learning, from the most elementary (knowledge) to its highest form.

According to Blum's taxonomy, the highest levels of learning involve both synthesis and evaluation, which requires the ongoing practice of self-reflection, which, begins with self-knowledge. As a coach, one encounters CEOs who have problems they cannot personally identify. If you can't see it, you sure won't be able to change it or fix it. Executives might lack the ability to fairly self-evaluate themselves and the dynamics of their surroundings. Coaching is guided by the task of providing new input to the CEO with the goal of having the CEO view his situation more clearly and consequently be better equipped to make the appropriate adjustments. The good news is the coach doesn't have an axe to grind. An executive coach is not driven by a need to be politically connected. The coach just wants the change that leads to better performance.

The coach is going to want to know everything possible about the CEO. If the CEO holds his cards tightly, this will be difficult. In initial sessions you'll want to be open about your personal and professional history. A good coach will ask about your early work experiences, how did you get started? Clearly, parents dramatically impact children in their formative years, and experience has taught me as a coach to explore the "table talk" that a leader experienced while growing up. What was discussed over dinner table in those formative years likely has had a huge influence on the leader's development. For example, entrepreneurs talk about future opportunities and thus help their children see how amazing it might be. Some families talk more about secure jobs, such as working in a union or for the government. I love hearing these stories, because they influence a leader's professional development.

Past or current entrepreneurial experiences provide a unique perspective. When left to their own desires, entrepreneurs tend to employ their true talents and strengths. Entrepreneurs normally have been forced to do a variety of jobs. When they had to step outside of their talents, they may have failed financially or fallen out of love with their business. They have typically dealt with both success and failure.

A coach will want to know about these experiences, which can leave scars or lead to positive adjustments. Question: How does the personal history relate to their present position? Have they figured out how to delegate, outsource, spin-off, or to grow by bringing on talent? These experiences create what I've labeled as "precedent constraints." They either influence a person to grow, or they create fear and may manifest in a desire for the status quo. Having this background information can be a true coaching opportunity.

A couple of small-scale examples: How might an entrepreneur be born? Necessity is the mother of invention. Many years ago in a short but sharp recession, a young man came to my door in the middle of the summer, saying that since work was hard to find, he was using number templates and spray-painting house numbers on curbs in front of houses in our subdivision. Intrigued, I asked, "After you paint my curb I will give you twenty dollars if you tell me how much you've made so far this summer." He said, "Let me paint the curb, you give me the twenty dollars, and I'll tell you." He'd made five thousand dollars in six weeks. Can you imagine the impact this had on his thinking both in the present and for the future?

Then I remember a student from Chicago who wanted to know what he could do in the lousy economy. I said, "Since you have some construction background, and you like using your hands, why not topcoat asphalt driveways?" He went for it. Later he came back to school for an additional semester, but he quit school because he was making so much money back home. He had a keen ability to manage unskilled workers. Do you have the talent to manage? According to Gallup, fewer than 10 percent of leaders do. Let's find out about you.

Your story might not be as entrepreneurial, but a coach will want to hear both inspiring—and not so inspiring—elements of your journey. Once you gained some footing, what jobs, or portions of jobs, did you enjoy? You'll be challenged to identify past successes to determine if the successes were a result of appropriately applied talent. Such conversations can help the interviewer see the executive's talent demonstrated in his or her past positions.

Keep in mind that every person is "a work in process." In the present, there are things that can be changed, improved, or dismissed. An experienced coach is a person who has likely spent a great deal of time assessing leaders. In that process, a good coach has also gained a high level of self-knowledge. The coach in collaboration with the CEO may find such topics can lead to fertile opportunities for positive change.

A coach who has mastered the evaluative process of self-reflection can serve a client well. The coach will know firsthand and thus be able to discuss the struggles and benefits associated with accepting one's limitations as well as refocusing one's talents. The message from the coach is "trust me; I get it." This leveling process between the coach and the CEO can be pivotal in setting a foundation of trust.

It is important to note that unsolicited input is rarely appreciated. A professional coach will stay on target. As noted, a coach who personally shares his or her story finds acceptance more easily. An excellent coach will make the strong personal connection that is needed to create an atmosphere where eventually the desire for input will be initiated by the CEO.

Such a coach inspires the CEO and is the CEO's

greatest fan and often most trusted confidant. It is easy to see why this happens. Imagine a talented coach whose primary purpose is to advance the CEO. What's not to like? Such advocacy should lead to positive organizational change.

Finally, the coach wishes to reduce the amount of distraction and stay on task. Distractions and negative branding don't advance the CEO. Working to achieve worthy goals is a benefit to the CEO and to his or her firm.

Change: Is It Positive or Negative?

Often people ask, what can destroy the coaching process? Finding out that a CEO is just going through the motions but is unwilling to change. The attitude, positive or negative, will demonstrate itself early in the coaching process. The coach must call it what it is and work toward establishing the authenticity discussed earlier.

One firm that I consulted demonstrated the idea very well. As we finalized our strategic marketing contract, one partner said to the other: "Okay, I signed the contract, and you'll get your damn plan."

I thought, *Oh no, this will be a disaster!* Fortunately the partner who wanted the marketing intervention decided that since his partner wasn't going to give it a chance, he would oversee the implementation process with my assistance. As a coach, my goal was to push the leader into experiences that helped him learn the basics of program implementation. The process went very well and the results were outstanding. The company is now one of the leading commercial builders in the central United States and is growing nationally.

A good coach will watch you in action and suggest changes based on perception. You might not be able to see your limitations or how they impact the organization. In my mind, limitations are not weaknesses but rather are based on talent that needs to be developed. A weakness is often a low-ranking talent that one endeavors to employ and consequently proves it is not her or his true talent.

Consider this example: As a young man, I was consulting a regional vice president in the largest nursing home company in the world. After facing years of crushing financial problems, this company was working through their third financial reorganization. My firm was hired to "mystery shop" (play the role of the customer) in nursing facilities in three states and consequently to create a strategic marketing program that would provide (a marketing) jump-start in the region.

After the assessment, I spoke at a meeting attended by nursing home directors from more than seventy facilities. The presentation went very well. People were excited about the possibility for change—a better service model. As I finished, the regional vice president came to the podium. "Phil, tremendous speech, and you were spot on." So far, so good. Then he told his people, "Phil is right, the fish stinks from the head down, and we are going to get rid of the rotten fish in this company." My attempt to set a positive tone went down the drain. As you can imagine, I had my work cut out for me with this man. He was clueless about or at least indifferent to—the negative effect of his communication on his organization. For this problem, coaching not consulting was needed.

This leader had been chosen to lead during a crisis situation, because his leadership approach was based on an "emergency" mind-set. So his tack was based on the idea that we will fix this very bad situation fast or "heads will roll." This commonly happens when there is an emergency situation. The problem was that his employees were already hurting emotionally, and insults didn't positively change the situation. Bottom line: limited self-awareness and limited ability to control emotions undermines many CEOs. It doesn't have to be that way!

I coached him about how to manage his thoughts and, therefore, his language. Language involves body language, spoken words, posture, verbal and facial inflection, and also the props we use when we speak. He learned how to soften his tone, so he would be heard but not perceived as threatening. He needed firm language with his managers.

A strong-minded CEO requires honest internal and external input that isn't politicized or watered down. The CEO must find out what is real and subsequently make recommendations accordingly. Leaders need someone at each level of the organization from top management, down to the janitors who will tell them the truth about how it feels to work in the organization and how the leader can make things better. Too many leaders don't understand and sometimes don't care how they impact the people who work for them, and that is not a way to create a healthy and profitable firm. Suggesting changes for a CEO can be seen as a threat or as a possibility for improvement. Open mindedness is very important. An essential question a CEO should ask is, how do others experience me?

Knowledgeable coaches will demonstrate how a negative policy or inappropriate communication impacts the organization or an individual. As a coach, I use a three-step model to demonstrate limitations. The model involves (1) principles, (2) pictures/visuals, and (3) applications. This is not rocket science but is quite revealing. We live in a visual world and pictures are very important. What someone sees and experiences each day in the work environment has a dramatic positive or negative impact.

Determining the guiding principles (see the model in the paragraph above) in a firm would include looking at personal and corporate goals: also what are the CEO's personal strengths and ethical values? Are these in the best interest of the company? Customers can inform us about whether these principles are played out in the larger marketplace. At the pictures/visual level, I help paint the picture and how it currently feels in the organization. Finally, the resulting ideas are applied so it is easy to see the results/ramifications. By looking at the results, the CEO will learn about the current reality, and by standing back and evaluating the process, the CEO will be better able to make positive changes.

The Coaching Landscape

Excellent coaches know when they should say yes and when

to say no. The long-term focus needs to be on the CEO's success and ultimately on the firm's success. At the beginning, the correct way to position a coaching engagement is to focus on the CEO, because the CEO is the one person who can have the most dramatic impact on the organization.

Once the benefits of the coach and CEO collaboration are clear, the CEO may desire a broader corporate involvement for the coach. A CEO may eventually ask the coach to work with the entire executive team. If this happens, a coach needs to clearly communicate how confidences and professional relationships will operate. A good coach will be meticulous in communicating how the process will work.

A coach who potentially gains "insider status" may believe this is workable for both the coach and the CEO, but if this takes place there is a danger for both; the coach as an insider becomes a de facto employee. Communication problems with others in the company can emerge.

People in the organization can easily become confused about the coach's role. If the organization moves a coach into a leadership position, the CEO should immediately announce such changes to those whose responsibilities will shift. Authority relationships and responsibilities need to be clarified. Where the coach, now executive, is placed on the organizational chart is the key. If the new executive (once a coach) is reporting to someone other than the CEO, such a change will need to be explained.

Normally, as the CEO, you should understand and

make it clear that the coach works exclusively for you. Although many coaches will do assessments, such as 360-feedback reports (involving input from a variety of sources including subordinates to paint a clear picture of CEO performance), the CEO controls the information flow. How CEOs decide to share the information with others in the organization is up to them.

Likewise, as CEO you'll want to ensure that your coach is fairly compensated. Economic equity-helps ensure that the coach will see no need to take credit for the CEO's successes. A good coach works behind the scenes. The coaching process is about the CEO's, and consequently the organization's, success.

If the coach is careful to protect privileged communication and is wise enough to let the CEO take credit for positive changes, the process of change will prove to be quite successful. The coach should leave his or her ego out of the process and simply prove the value of collaborative coaching, improved decision-making, and flawless implementation.

Even in a crisis, the coach helps the CEO by facilitating thoughtful decision-making, often pointing the CEO to appropriate resources, including talented people who can help. Additionally, a good coach will ensure the CEO backs away from the abyss of ethically questionable actions. This will work if the coach's ethical boundaries were clarified during the hiring process. The coach is a collaborator in the finest sense of the word.

A Coaching Process

To wrap up this chapter, I offer a concise summary of the coaching process, though we haven't yet thoroughly discussed all these elements. There's more to come in chapter 3.

Introductions

The initial meeting between the CEO and the coach is intended to begin the process of building a positive relationship. It is also to determine the CEO's readiness to start the coaching process and to determine initial points of focus. A responsible case for coaching is established. Often the introductory meeting is referred to as a "Chemistry Meeting."

Assessment

A CEO assessment process is undertaken to provide a foundation for the coaching process. This assessment involves in-depth interviews, and typically a top-management 360-evaluation is performed. Occasionally CEO shadowing is recommended, and an effort is made to determine organizational values. In addition, initial corporate atmosphere and culture assessments are made. Typically a simple industry analysis will also be undertaken to ensure the coach is aware of industry dynamics. Finally, a confidentiality agreement is created and agreed to by both parties.

Analysis

In the analysis process, the coach combines the assessment details and outlines the CEO's competencies and strengths. Also, there is a thorough discussion of findings and the stage is set for a positive, collaborative, coaching process. In the end, the coach and the CEO secure agreement about areas to focus on for improvement and key goals to target. The coach needs to understand and keep in mind the need for positive business results—that the organization must advance financially to help legitimize the resources earmarked for the coaching engagement.

Plans and Objectives

An initial CEO leadership development plan is established. Areas of coaching focus on measurable goals, organizational positioning, vision casting, and stakeholder involvement, interpersonal communication skills, CEO leadership style, conflict resolution, planning skills, decision-making skills, thematic business communication, personal branding, motivation skills, listening skills, and so on.

Implementation

Finally, the implementation process is underway. The coach and CEO focus on developing the CEO's strengths. The CEO's level of engagement in his or her work is extremely important. There is a need to determine "off-setters," that is, people or processes to offset the CEO's limitations. This process ultimately ensures there will be additional time for the CEO to efficiently employ his or her realized strengths. A determination is made about resources that are available for CEO development. Appropriate timelines and measurement techniques are implemented. Plans for feedback and reporting are determined. Even at the implementation stage, analysis and reflection continue. Those "how could we have handled that differently?" debriefings can lead to positive results, and over time the results can be quite remarkable. Consider Peter Drucker's insightful comment: "Follow effective action with quiet reflection. From the quiet reflection will come even more effective action" (as quoted in *The Definitive Drucker*).

Conclusion

Great coaches are often viewed like excellent teachers; a CEO never forgets the memorable lessons these coaches provide. Occasionally these lessons transcend the moment and greatly change a CEO's organizational impact. Long-term relationships between coaches and CEOs often result.

One of my clients has employed my coaching and consulting services for twenty-plus years. For me the relationship always about advancing the client and his business, but, over time, it became personal. As a result, the friendship has led to years of mutual concern even to the point of attending each other's major life events. Such a coaching relationship reminds me of what one of my favorite teachers used to say. "Teaching is a privilege and not a right. Treat it as such!"

As another example that demonstrates the value of great coaching, a recent Netflix program involved the 1985 Super Bowl–winning Chicago Bears. In 1985 the "bad boys" of the Chicago team were unstoppable. In the program it was easy to be touched, noting the lifelong influence of Buddy Ryan on so many of his players. Whether you approved of Ryan's methods or not, he created one of the finest defenses ever to take the field. Great teachers and coaches never fade in the minds of those whose lives changed because of their influence.

In summary, if the CEO is employing his or her talents 55 percent of the time, and the coach can help the CEO achieve 80 to 85 percent engagement, the CEO's paradigm shifts. Aided by good advice in reference to systems and personnel and further assisted by the wise use of outside resources, the entire paradigm will positively change. Implemented correctly, the bottom line will improve as well. The coach will have provided an outstanding return on investment for the services performed.

Chapter 3

Time and Talents: Priorities and Stewardship

We've covered a lot of ground already, but let's look at a few more practical questions a coach can ask—and help you answer. Many coaches encourage the wise stewardship of time and talents. These are two distinct elements central to our work and personal life, but they are related to each other in more ways than their alliterative names.

Is This the Best Use of My Time?

Everyone knows that time cannot be inventoried or reused. So every CEO should consider the key question, how am I using my time? In helping you determine what your primary focus should be, a coach would address time management issues. How and when can you either dispose of (if possible) or delegate the tasks you do not do well? How can company leaders work in concert with you to multiply your positive impact? This can help to minimize your involvement with a task that is a lousy fit. This process sounds easy, but it can be quite challenging. If this process were easy, you would have already mastered it.

As you pursue what you enjoy doing—employing your talents—continually ask, is this task a good use of my time? Is it below my pay grade? Do I have true talent in this area? If not, what talent is missing? Then I need to find a person who possessed that talent. You can't do this unless you know what the other person brings to the table.

For example, when consulting a company for an extended period of time, I was unable to convince the CEO, whose expertise was finance and accounting, to focus on important issues (many of which he had skill to deal with). The ongoing financial constraints facing the company were complicated by the CEO's reluctance to focus on the most important issues. In the end, he proved that number crunching could not solve all problems, and soon he was cutting into the flesh and bones of his firm. What was needed was process enhancements and marketing, and he did not want to enlist people to help with those areas, which were out of his purview. If this executive had been open to change, a coach could have pushed him to expand his thinking and refocus corporate resources. For those efforts, the risks seemed too high. In this case, my ideas were appreciated but rarely implemented in a way that truly advanced the company.

The issue of priorities is a key part of the coach's attention. You have heard that most CEOs are workaholics. Many feel that certain tasks cannot be done well by others. The coach will want to help the CEO tweak what she does in terms of work tasks, how she ensures the work is done well, whom she involves in the process, what tasks she delegates, and what she is or might be willing to outsource.

Simple question: As a leader were you a workaholic on the way up through the ranks? Was that an expectation driven by those above you, or was it based on your attitude about your job? Could you have made better decisions about using supporting staff during the various stages of your career? I have always operated on the idea that a CEO's primary role is to duplicate him or herself. Honestly grade yourself as to how you did when it came to developing the talent in others. I'm not talking about building a bureaucracy, but I am talking about building strong teams. A coach helps leaders think through the process of leadership—how to manage and motivate the team—and pushes the CEO to gain knowledge related to planning and expansion, and so forth. Time is the one input that cannot be inventoried; once it is spent it cannot be retrieved.

One helpful time-management method is evaluating the time spent on legitimate CEO responsibilities. A coach tracks a CEO's time to see if he is doing the five-hundred-dollar-per-hour work or the five-dollar-per-hour work. I often focus the conversation on financial contribution to the success of the company. Don't misread this, because some of the most important time is one-on-one with employees and customers. A coach does this well when he keeps the CEO's talent clearly in focus, helping to use it more effectively.

Executive excellence requires self-knowledge as well as discipline—to work efficiently but also to know that balance is better than burnout. A recent book written by Robert Gates, who worked for both Democrats and Republicans in a variety of key positions including Secretary of Defense and Director of the Central Intelligence Agency, made the point well. Gates noted that he never worked on a Saturday! Do you know any CEO who doesn't occasionally (or often) work Saturdays (and probably Sundays)? The discipline needed to have a personal life is hard to accomplish. The self-control to use time wisely is invaluable. Stephen Covey was correct, in *The 7 Habits of Highly Effective People*, saying that CEOs should "do first things first."

Listening to Needs

Most coaches agree that CEOs need to spend more time with their customers. Customers will help you see what is "authentic and true" about your organization. Many CEOs feel that keeping their customers out of their offices enables them to complete what is often called "the real work." Partly true, but an over commitment to internal issues can quickly lead the CEO to becoming out of touch. Results happen outside the organization in the marketplace and not inside of the company. Great coaches consistently help to refocus CEOs to achieve results.

Think in terms of a newly established small business. Even a casual observer would notice that most small businesses open their doors, start to prosper financially, and consequently decide to never change a thing. This is because they are operating based on a seemingly "unending limited perspective." Their mantra is "if it isn't broke, don't fix it." The lack of collaboration usually results in stagnation. One consequence of stagnation is that talented people who desire a positive career path go elsewhere.

A couple of fast-food restaurants prove the point nicely. When Taco Bell learned about price elasticity in the

1970s, they lowered their prices, and their volume and profitability dramatically increased. But they still build those tiny stores. Don't they realize it is fine to build a bigger store? Likewise Dairy Queen decided early that napkins should be small. Apparently, they never saw a small child eat ice cream. I'm relatively sure most parents would vote for bigger napkins.

It is surprising how many smaller companies haven't figured out how technology has changed the landscape in terms of their business. If you don't know your customers, and you don't listen to your employees, and you don't keep up on technological changes, why would you ever consider changing the ways you do business? You're certainly not going to take input from a coach. I learned early that failing companies are typically the last to ask for help. Companies that have plateaued, in terms of growth, are the ones who are the quickest to seek outside help from coaches and consultants.

A team approach is a tremendous way to break down the barriers associated with "small thinking." The multiple inputs from participating team members tend to wake the leadership to the idea that many answers can be found simply by listening. If we can agree that collaboration is an indispensable benefit related to teams, would such collaboration between a CEO and coach be any different? I think not.

The influence of "human nature" means CEOs (in fact, all people) tend to focus on what they enjoy and often place the weightier issues on the "back burner." A coach will help a CEO find positive off-setters, people and systems to take up the slack in areas where CEOs lack the relevant talent needed to excel. The focus of the coach is to sharpen the focus of CEO talent to maximize the effectiveness of processes and communication.

If a CEO struggles with being warm, he or she can lean on others to create warmth. One university president who was not well equipped to warm up an audience used me on a regular basis to speak (put a friendly comedian on stage first), and then we would facilitate a Q and A. I helped him learn to share from his heart. I worked with him to be more transparent, more extroverted, to be the first to extend a hand, to stay closer to people, to manage by what Tom Peters termed "management by walking around"—a casual technique in which an executive frequently walks through the facility, talking and observing employees; it engages people at all levels throughout an organization, to gather input about how a firm could improve. A side benefit is that the face-to-face interaction gives people a voice, promoting better performance.

What Can I Learn from Outsiders?

Without having collaboration with others, a CEO's perspective is based primarily on personal experience—education, training, relationships, and current context. One hopes that parents, teachers, colleagues, and faith leaders have enhanced the development of positive moral principles.

Reading is one helpful tool to expand horizons and see new possibilities, but exploration is even better. Coaches often use field trips to break down barriers to new creative thinking. Never underestimate the value of the new ideas and fresh images that a business field trip can provide. A field trip can be anything from a simple trip to a nonrelated industry, an afternoon visit to a movie, a visit to a regional TED talk, or an off-site educational event. The field trip can be a positive mini-shock treatment to help a CEO and other leaders expand their vision. Every field trip should require a debriefing/application session that helps participants talk about the difference the trip could potentially make for their organization.

Many years ago one of my university colleagues made his first trip to an Apple Computer store. When he saw how crowded the store was, the staff's use of handheld inventory/accounting devices, and the inventory management system, his mind was blown. Nothing is more effective in stirring the mind than experiencing a new reality. I looked at him and said, "Why can't every business learn something about business process from experiencing this?" He agreed wholeheartedly.

When working with medical personnel, one of my favorite educational tools was a movie called *The Doctor* (we will call it an in-house field trip). The key star is William Hurt, who displays horrible customer service and a shockingly rude bedside manner. As the plot progresses, he finds out he has cancer, thus himself becoming the patient. Face it, sooner or later everyone gets sick. The movie has an amazing ability to wake up nursing home and hospital personnel about the need to demonstrate heartfelt care as they do their jobs.

When working with others, executives lean heavily (far too much) on their own professional experience. Such an approach can quickly lead subordinates to alter their input to fit the CEO's perspective. The resultant danger is "groupthink." For example, it's been widely reported that Centcom (United States Central Command) would dumb down intelligence information for President Obama to fit his view that the war on terror was being won. The political world is powerfully influenced and driven by groupthink, defined by Merriam-Webster as "a pattern of thought characterized by self-deception, forced manufacture of consent, and conformity to group values and ethics." Being a captive of the organization changes interpersonal dynamics. Again, a coach needs to be independent and free of much of what insiders must deal with especially as it relates to ethics—which we'll discuss in a later chapter.

A classic economic example demonstrates paradigmatic thinking and how it affects, maybe hamstrings, political leaders. Democrats believe the way to increase federal government revenue is to increase taxes. Republicans think reducing taxes will create incentives and bring in more revenue. Both have their entrenched interest groups writing the checks to ensure the paradigm never changes. In reality, research indicates that Democrats are correct if one is considering the short-term, and Republicans are correct if one is considering the long-term. True leadership rarely emerges when systems are stuck in a closed paradigm.

A closed paradigm is one where disagreement is not allowed. Every healthy organization sees the benefit of healthy disagreement and new perspectives. If everyone simply follows the leader, never sharing new perspectives, the company quickly gets out of touch with reality. Such an organization is easy pickings for a fast-moving, customer-oriented, listening competitor.

But as a positive example I think of Thomas Edison. If opportunity arises, visit Edison's labs and winter home in Fort Myers, Florida. Edison was clearly a man of energy, genius, and focus. He was constantly looking around the world for new materials, new ideas, and for inspiration. Still, it is true that very few notable accomplishments rise and fall based solely on the contributions of one individual.

Many great innovators visited Edison to work out various product issues. They thrived on a collaborative, team approach. Henry Ford accomplished much as a result of Edison's ongoing encouragement. Ford and Edison perfected great ideas working in concert with each other. For automobiles, Edison helped Ford with electrical and lighting elements. Ford brought Edison new cars, many still on display at his Florida home. Harvey Firestone was also a collaborator with these two giants. Firestone and Edison made the first automobile tires out of latex made from goldenrod. There is no such thing as a solitary man or a self-made genius. Anyone you can think of who fits this description probably acted effectively based on personal strengths and was likely gifted enough to see, appreciate, and thus employ the strengths of others.

Stewardship of Coaching Talent

In chapter 2, I listed five "best uses" of coaching talent. We've looked at the first use—helping a CEO become effective and efficient. Before delving into organizational concerns, I want to address the fifth use, "to work with struggling top executives," in terms of stewardship of time and resources. You'll note I said, never make this your focus. Unfortunately many CEOs believe that coaches should be hired primarily to deal with problem executives. But a negative stigma often associated with coaching is a result of coaches' taking on these tasks. It is widely accepted that 80 percent of management time is wasted on the bottom 20 percent of personnel regarding their performance.

So why hire a coach or consultant to double down on this proven pattern of failure? Focusing the coach on negatives versus positives is a misallocation of coaching resources. All this is to say that hiring a coach to focus primarily on underperforming subordinates is a mistake. In the end, others in leadership will wonder if they are next in line for remedial coaching. But after working with the CEO, a coach could well be tasked with helping the good performers become outstanding performers. Sorting out talent and helping to refocus the CEO will iron out many of the problems with the firm's low performers.

In the end, the CEO may well decide that the marginal executive needs to leave, especially if that person is negatively influencing the entire team. Occasionally putting a bandage on a minor personnel problem may work. On the other hand, if the CEO takes responsibility for discouraging a subordinate or placing that person in a wrong talent fit, a coach may be able to sort that out. But if the coach takes the assignment of remedially coaching a subordinate leader, the result will often mean both the coach and the problem executive will get fired.

Again, coaches don't fire people. They should not have line decision-making responsibilities. Better for the CEO to make a "go" or "no-go" decision about the struggling executive based on reliable sources of information.

Additionally, a coach should rarely push for the dismissal of a leader. Doing so will quickly give the coach the reputation of being a "hit man" for the executive team, and the negative "branding" could destroy the coach's ability to serve the firm. It can also destroy potential coaching engagements with potential future clients. A coach needs to remain above the fray.

A practical albeit unrealistic analogy: Suppose a person had $1 million to invest. One investment projects a statistically safe 1 percent return, and a contrasting investment for the $1 million projects a statistically safe 40 percent return. Would it be prudent to put money in the investment that is likely to have the lowest return? I think not. Likewise, coaching should direct attention on where the impact—the return of investment—will be the greatest.

The coach should help a CEO understand his or her potential impact.

Wrap-Up

Athletic competition provides an excellent example of why coaching is so essential. Great coaches facilitate outstanding athletic performance. Think of the great quarterbacks in the NFL. Would Joe Montana, Terry Bradshaw, Tom Brady, or Peyton Manning ever have reached such a high level of success without coaches? Even today, the majority of talented CEOs are slow to (in Stephen Covey's words "sharpen the saw") carefully work on their professional development. There never seems to be time for professional development.

Athletes understand the need for professional development. The coach is an ever-present reality consistently pushing for better results. Peyton Manning noted, upon the announcement of his retirement after eighteen successful years in the NFL, that the first thing he did was contact all his past coaches to thank them—a tremendous testimony of the value one gains from using coaches. And who was a more serious "learner" than Peyton Manning? Who showed more leadership or took more responsibility for failure than Peyton? At his retirement, he also recognized all the great role models he looked up to including Johnny Unitas, Joe Montana, and Dan Marino. What a testimony to coaching.

Although a simplistic example, how quickly a coach can bring about change is exemplified by dieting. If you try to change all your bad habits at once, you will fail. Coaches look for early changes that can create dramatic results.

Success will motivate the executive to try even

more. When coaches work with young executives, the changes come more quickly. It is more challenging to secure changes in a person who has had a good amount of success by doing it in Frank Sinatra mode: "my way." Learning is easier when one approaches it with humility rather than with arrogance.

The key is to focus coaching energy on the changes that will lead to the most significant improvements for both the CEO and the organization.

Chapter 4

Sharpen and Perfect Your Strengths

- Currently could you list your talents and explain how your organization benefits by having you as a leader?
- Have you ever asked others to list your strengths?

In chapter 2, we noted that the first of five "best uses" of an executive coach is to help the CEO become more effective and efficient. A coach facilitates this process by helping a client turn talents into strengths.

The good news is that God did not shortchange humans when it came to providing them with talent. Each person has talents that when fully realized and developed lead to strengths. Strengths represent the foundation for every accomplishment. So, I ask two key questions: (1) how does one discover one's personal talents? and (2) how does one build those talents into strengths?

Some notable authors have written books focused on the need to build jobs around individual strengths. Notably, the late Peter Drucker discussed the importance of focusing on strengths. This theme surfaced in many of his books, especially *The Effective Executive*. Later the work of Gallup scientists in concert with Dr. Don Clifton and Tom Rath developed the Clifton StrengthsFinder assessment, introduced in chapter 1.

Many of the most iconic CEOs in America followed their hearts (talents) from very early in their lives. Think of an accomplished CEO whom you admire. Got that person locked in your mind? When you think about that person's success, what is paramount in your thinking? Talent! Weakness rarely delivers success.

Warren Buffett, from the time he was a boy, loved business and numbers. Early in his life, he knew he would make a large deal of money. Buffett has an uncanny ability to focus on the details that enabled him to know what he should invest in next. Berkshire Hathaway is the result of Mr. Buffett's talent. He followed his heart—that is, what he loved to do—and became one of the richest men in the world. I'm quite sure Mr. Buffett didn't just keep doing the job, but rather found hundreds of ways to do it better; that is what developing talents into strengths is all about. Often referred to as the Oracle, Mr. Buffett had a talent that allowed him to focus on the analytical details and build them into the strengths that led to phenomenally successful investing.

Some young people, maybe even you, take longer to identify and act on their talents. Many parents, for example, push children toward "safe" jobs that don't suit them temperamentally. Some parents, living vicariously through their children, drive them to choose careers such as theirs. As a teacher, I was coaching a gifted young woman with a winning people-oriented temperament. If you are familiar with the StrengthsFinder assessment, you would understand if I said, "Julie had Woo" (short for "winning others over"). Julie always had an inviting smile and a kind word. She was extremely popular and well known on campus. Additionally Julie was gifted in art, in music, in design, and, to my assessment, a naturally gifted (instinctive) marketer.

It didn't take long for me to notice that Julie resisted my career recommendations. She kept repeating, "I'm going to be an attorney." I reflected on my own college experience, taking some law courses. I had realized that law wasn't for me, and Julie's talents and temperament were much like mine. I could not understand why Julie felt that law was her desired destiny. Finally, one day I had heard enough. I said, "Julie, you are not going to be an attorney." She said, "Why do you say that?" This led to several questions from me that were followed by quick responses from her:

Phil	Julie
Let me guess, you are from Michigan, maybe from Detroit?	Yes
And your father is a successful attorney?	Yes
And your father works in a top position for an automobile company?	Yes
And your father is pushing you to become an attorney?	Yes

Next I asked, "Why all the intensity from your father?

She said, "Dad had failed at a few things before he pursued law. He has had great success in law and feels a legal career would provide both an interesting job and an excellent income for me. He is doing this all out of love. Dad doesn't want me to struggle. He's a great guy."

I said, "In my mind, it is wrong for your father to live vicariously through you. He may not even know he is doing it. Do you think you can tell him that?"

Julies said, "It's pretty complicated. You see, at first he pressured my older sister to pursue law. She tried, and she hated it. She flat refused to go down that path. Now, I'm the next one in line."

I continued, "Julie you can't let someone else live your life, not even your father. You have remarkable talents, but they aren't helpful in the kind of profession your dad is pushing for. Have the conversation with your father."

Julie told me that they subsequently worked it all out. When Julie and her husband (later to become a pastor) left college, they worked as dorm parents for a different university. Eventually they pursued mission work in Mexico. She helped with the fund raising (putting those marketing skills to work) and became the communications point person who consistently presented to supporters her family's ministry to the poor.

Whether you've been quick or slow to act on your talents, there is still room to develop them into strengths.

Developing Talents into Strengths

It would be nearly impossible to write about coaching without using the words *talent* and *strength*. The following definitions have been established by Gallup researchers: "A strength is the ability to consistently provide near-perfect performance in a specific activity. Talents are naturally recurring patterns of thought, feeling, or behavior that can be productively applied. Talents, knowledge, and skills—along with the time spent (i.e., investment) practicing, developing your skills, and building your knowledge base—combine to create your strengths." (http://www.strengthsquest.com/help/general/143096/difference-talent-strength.aspx)

Talent exists in each person, but strength comes from developing those talents. Malcolm Gladwell popularized the idea that it took ten thousand hours of practice to master a skill. (Many others debate the estimate.) Does it take ten thousand hours to convert talent into a legitimate strength? God only knows. But one thing for sure: developing and applying talent is the path to gaining a legitimate strength.

I again recommend that you take the StrengthsFinder assessment and evaluate your top five and then top ten talents. Do they resonate with what you know about yourself? I'll address this again in a later chapter; for now I note that StrengthsFinder is not an assessment to look at once or twice and then set aside. It takes time, commitment, collaboration, and trust to understand and apply the information at a deeper level.

So how does one develop talents into strengths? For starters, look for ways that allow your talents to be exposed and, therefore, on full display. When the compliments start coming, it is a good early indication that you are using your talents. This can showcase your talents to leaders and board members who control resources that could be expended to maximize the talent. As time passes, colleagues will see your talent and likely encourage you to employ it as much as possible. One established writer I know doesn't have a typical English or writing degree. But when she turned her hand to writing, the affirmation she received from colleagues prompted her to hone her craft. Using your talents helps you perfect your talents. Education and related experiences can certainly help in this regard.

Pursue experiences and gain the knowledge and training that polishes and perfects your talent. In my own experience, students and clients began complimenting me about my creative approaches to teaching and in business (ideation at work). I think it happens to most people as they begin to focus on their talents. In business clients began recommending that I join certain community and ministry boards to help infuse new ideas.

My first real "business" boss gave me projects that would advance the company, and most were built around new ideas. Next, I found he was flying me to different cities to learn about property development. Eventually, I would build programs to help cities turn failing downtown districts into retail successes. If I was left to my own creativity, good things happened. That carried over into consulting, as my ideas helped break industry paradigms. I learned how to harness ideas that worked in one industry and apply the same methods to unrelated industries. I loved marketing and business. I spent as much time as I could to develop a deeper understanding of these areas.

In my view, it is in smaller organizations that the process of developing one's strengths happens more rapidly. A wide variety of tasks are left to CEOs, who no doubt gravitate to what they enjoy, which usually means their talent base. If there is no job description, a CEO will normally develop one built around her own personal talents and strengths. CEOs take short executive training courses at notable universities. They spend time with others in their industry. In my view, the sharpest CEOs find value in learning from others who lead in unrelated industries.

Even if a CEO doesn't consciously know her talents, as time unfolds talent-oriented outcomes will be observable to others. As one tries new things outside of work, she will stick with the ones that logically prove true competence. If people are enjoying some measure of success, it is likely because they were using their talent and strengths.

Embracing Personal Growth

How much time do you set aside for self-development and reflection? CEOs often don't relish taking the time needed to develop their talents. Stephen Covey was right, that "sharpening the saw" (learning and developing talent and skills) doesn't get the attention it deserves. Clearly education is intended to bring about change, and training is intended to provide a quick return on investment. When I go to training, I immediately try to apply what I learned the next day. A university for which I worked was successful at securing contracts with a variety of business and community organizations so employees could complete their MBAs. Virtually every firm I worked with has indicated that the money spent for these advanced degrees was well worth the dollar investment.

It would be impossible for me as a coach if I had to say, "Let's do the hard work associated with coaching but the benefits will be negligible." Thankfully, this is not the case with coaching. CEOs admit coaching is worth the resources expended as the firm enjoys renewed financial success.

Think about someone who has already impacted your life. For me, my father played a pivotal role. Sometimes others make a difference. A friend in leadership gave me a jewel when he said, "Phil if someone pays you a compliment. You should return the compliment with a compliment." So if someone says, "Nice job." You could say, "Thanks for being so kind." Wonderful idea.

As CEO, you need to reflect about your responsibilities as both the quarterback and the coach for your organization. For example, are you truly developing your people? Excellent coaching demonstrates to CEOs how they, in fact, should be developing their people. The most significant effort you can expend is the time spent on conceptual work. This is easy to accomplish when "reflection" is built into the organizational planning process. Unfortunately most CEOs spend far less time focusing on conceptual work than they should. Too often the tyranny of the moment rules, yes, tyrannically.

Conceptual work is the time given to learning, reflecting, and strategically thinking about things such as sustainability and long-range success. The future is advanced by the full development of people—including oneself—coupled with careful consideration of growth opportunities, supported by research and planning. If you dislike playing the role of the visionary, you had better have a visionary on your top management team. Conceptual thinking will allow you to see these opportunities emerge.

CEOs often enjoy the "doing," or implementing, but the reflecting (non-doing) drives them insane. Doers have a difficult time making time for research, thinking, and reflection. Being busy is not the same as doing the truly significant work—which can begin with discovering ways to hone your strengths. You need people with the talents you lack to help your team perform.

A family analogy can drive the point home. A parent becomes a better parent by asking, what does my child need from me at this point in life? A spouse becomes a better spouse by backing away from a situation and honestly asking, in what ways did I contribute to the problem? As the Bible states, "…first cast out the beam out of thine own eye; and then shalt thou see clearly to cast out the mote out of thy brother's eye" KJV (Matthew 7:5). Reflection involves offering vulnerability so meaningful collaboration can take place. When we open up to others, the consequential give-and-take can provide in dramatic results.

Now apply the analogy to the job of being a CEO. A CEO has to be creative and take risks. Doing so without significant input will likely lead to failure. For example, if you have never taken a business nationwide, getting input from those who have done so would be helpful. In summary, the key is being open to input, reflection, and collaboration and keeping those bureaucratic tendencies from leading to less-than-desirable decisions.

So is it easy to make time and "space" to pursue conceptual work? Not so much. The tyranny of the moment can overwhelm anyone. Putting out fires and dealing with short-term problems can give one a feeling of accomplishment. One sometimes needs coaching help to find the appropriate balance between time spent on short-term needs and working to accomplish the big goals. On the first page of his book *The Tyranny of Time,* Robert Banks notes, "Your view of time and use of it will tell me more about you, and you more about yourself, than almost anything else." A good coach will push CEOs to sharpen their conceptual skills, to seek significant input, and to keep their eyes on the horizon.

Getting in the Flow

By carefully developing one's talents and perfecting them into strengths, one can ultimately make a significant difference in the world. Additionally, an individual will be fully alive (loving and being competent in his or her work) when fully using personal talents. In teaching, this feeling is called "getting in the flow."

President Ronald Reagan created his political career based a well-defined list of beliefs. He believed communism was a totalitarian system that was both "evil" and unworkable as an economic system. Reagan also believed the government was too big and therefore responsible for the lackluster 1970s US economic performance. He was staunchly prolife and pro-family. He would not compromise on these values. Additionally, President Reagan had the ability to communicate these ideas in ways the average citizen could clearly understand. He was a simple man with simple beliefs and marvelous communication skills. I'm guessing the "belief" talent drove him to stay the course. President Reagan employed his convictions and his ability to communicate, and he changed the world. He honed his talent on radio, in the movies, in speaking for General Electric Theater, and by making hundreds of political speeches.

When people are fully using their true talents and strengths, it will be evident to onlookers. Steve Jobs was a CEO admired by many, though his journey took several unexpected turns. If you were a fan of Apple Computer, you have likely read, watched, and learned about Steve Jobs, often referred to as the "high priest" of emerging technologies. Fans know that Steve Jobs' friend Steve Wozniak was involved in a group of computer/electronic hobbyists named the Homebrew Computer Club. A tremendous amount of creativity came from that group.

Later Wozniak and Jobs launched Apple Computer. After successfully launching Apple, Jobs was eventually forced out by the board and by John Sculley. Imagine being forced out of a successful organization you founded. After a period of reflection, coming to terms with being publicly fired, Jobs started NeXT. Although relatively unsuccessful, later NeXT technologies became the basis of the famous OS operating system driving Apple Computer today. I believe NeXT is the word that clearly describes Steve Jobs' business DNA. He was curious, inventive, imaginative, and a super tinkerer. Someone once said, "In Steve Jobs' mind lies the future." What a generous comment about Jobs' talent; he was a futurist, a person gifted with brilliant, visionary ideas. He was not an angel, but Apple benefited by letting him work his strengths.

Peter Drucker noted, "Managers do things right; leaders do the right thing." *The Effective Executive* (1967). The "right things" are going to be most successful if the CEO is using his or her strengths to pursue and implement them.

Learn to Say Yes and No

Don't use talent as a scapegoat, but it is important to understand that when you are not working based on talent and strengths, it will impact your attitude, the quality of your work, and it can certainly add stress.

The key is to say yes to tasks and responsibilities that allow you to use your talent. If possible, say no to tasks and responsibilities that don't allow you to use your talent. It will never be perfect, but the goal is to hit 80-plus percent fit where you clearly have talent. As you turn talents into strengths, look to your organization for help: What can your board and your subordinates do, and what training, education, and experiences are available to help you operate at the optimum level?

The goal of subordinates is to multiply the strengths of those above them. Obviously, they will have to understand their leader's talent and strengths and vice versa. This vice versa is a key to recalibrating an organization for strengths, the topic of our next chapter.

Chapter 5

Recalibrating for Strengths

Many CEOs lack the knowledge needed to build a strengths-based organization. CEOs often don't develop and engage the latent talent that currently resides in their employees. Most successful hiring comes from employing the trial-and-error method. Unfortunately, such a process wastes precious resources, both human and financial. Additionally, such an approach often hurts the people who inevitably get caught in the spokes via unfavorable hiring and training methods.

Nigel Piercy, in his excellent book *Market-Led Strategic Change: Transforming the Process of Going to Market*, stated, "Hidden assets in the business are strengths which are lying dormant." Brilliant. Think about your organization. Too often human talent is hidden in plain sight. If it helps, state the problem in financial terms. If employees are only 20 percent engaged, rather than an optimal 80-plus percent engaged, the organization is vastly underutilizing its talent. Additionally, the employees are likely to be unhappy in their work.

Are employees fired for moral indiscretion, for breaking the sacred ethical codes of your organization, or for missing work? If not, they may be fired because a job description forces them to misapply talent. The truly immoral act may be exemplified by wrongly firing a person because the leadership hasn't positioned the person based on talent.

Commonly CEOs make an attempt to fix the problems associated with an ineffective employee. Human resource personnel will attempt to retrain the employee, scheduling obligatory one-on-one conferences in an attempt to help the employee. They likely will follow due process on the path to letting the employee go. But look at it objectively, the entire process may be a result of human resource personnel not finding the appropriate talent fit for the employee.

Unfortunately, this scenario plays out over and over again. Note: excellent coaches will refuse to participate in corporate reorganizations that are actually shrouded attempts to get rid of people. Except for extreme financial difficulties, major moral indiscretions, or seismic technological reverberations, letting people go is often due to hiring mistakes made by the firm.

It is both frustrating and challenging for employees to spend their professional lives working outside of their talents. If you hear someone telling you how many years they have until retirement, it may be a strong indication they are working outside of their talents. In my experience, I hear this most from governmental employees. And far too often firms abuse the employees they see as ineffective, incompetent, or lackluster in terms of work ethic.

Old Paradigm: The Behavioral School of Management

Business often gets it wrong when it comes to understanding talent. In teaching, I often talked about what I've labeled the

"Behavioral School of Management" versus the "Strengths School of Management." If one is in the wrong job, with the wrong people, in the wrong town, very soon the person will feel that the compensation isn't enough. The Behavioral School model—which has been the focal point of graduate business education for several decades—has placed many in those bad-fit positions and tried diligently to reform the employees. The underlying assumptions are that with job descriptions, training, modeling, incentives, and sometimes with strange interventions, one can ultimately change a person to fit the job description. The goal of the Behavioral School of Management it is to "remake" people. This is the opposite of building talents and strengths and therefore counters a goal of employee engagement.

Organizations seem to feel that job descriptions give them more control (easier path to remaking people) over how things get done, but they are not effective. Job descriptions (1) are typically not based on employee or applicant talent and strengths but rather on the preconceived needs of the organization; (2) are for management's convenience, not oriented toward efficiency; (3) are usually tied to performance evaluations (if you are 50 percent engaged in your job, a 60 percent performance rating, in reality, might be an A+).

If particular employees looked at their current job descriptions, most would say, this description is not even close to what I do. Thankfully, in the past two decades, human resource people have been more accurate with placement, because there is normally a significant amount of assessment before someone is hired. Still, how can a job description accurately account for all the change that a position is subjected to today?

Sometimes by chance, trial and error works out; the job description happens to be a fit. And sometimes people win the lottery. Other times people sell themselves into jobs that are not a fit. Very often these people were desperate and, therefore, will take a job that will put food on the table.

But what will be the end results? Can one expect engagement at work by employing this hit-or-miss methodology? Can one expect a person to perform at a high level in a position that doesn't fit personal strengths? Can one expect the typical job in such an organization to be free of frustration? Will the job ensure some level of happiness at work? Will an employee's blood pressure continue to stay in the normal range?

For example, most executives have witnessed companies endeavoring to keep their people-oriented employees locked away and securely grounded in their cubicles. Unfortunately, the little rascals sneak out so they can be with people, thus using the talents that are relational in nature. What an incredible waste of talent and financial resources.

Example 2: A public relations CEO hired only female employees (rather curious and very likely illegal) to write public relations releases but would not let them speak to one another during the workday. Policing these conversations became a monumental task. One woman reported that she needed therapy after working for that CEO.

Let your mind reflect on this idea: how many people do you think have been reprimanded or fired, not because they lacked talent, but because of low performance caused by a "bad job fit"? Many firms are amazed when these same employees perform extremely well in competing companies (or in different positions within the same organization). Occasionally it is a result of the new firm beginning with a good discussion about talent, conversations about what worked for the employee in the past, and so on.

Most young people change jobs frequently. Many assume they are in the wrong field or that they took the wrong major in college. Some believe their parents were right; they just don't like to work. Leaving college and adjusting to the "real world" does take time. But often the problem is a bad fit based on talent and corporate culture.

Consequences of Misapplied Talent

Expensive Turnover

When they misapply talent or hire the wrong people, executives quickly learn that turnover is very expensive. I think of my early experience at Prudential, where a huge bureaucracy seemed willing to deal with the turnover associated with the misapplication of talent. The field sales agents had challenging jobs. Selling life insurance was difficult; in those days Prudential salespeople were not selling securities. Whole-life insurance was a tough sell. If you were dying, you couldn't buy it, and if you were in perfect health, you'd see no need for it. Success required real sales talent. The average twenty-four-month retention rate of agents was 21 percent. Trial and error wasn't and isn't a very efficient way to hire.

Look at the turnover issues on a more local level. Even at a fast-food restaurant, it is evident that employees take on a broad array of job responsibilities. Some of these tasks an employee will do well—but not all. Consequently the employee might be let go, or he might vote with his feet and leave. Chances are, there will be little or no legal action. Let's say it is hard to get people to apply for these jobs. Sometimes the restaurant's only option is to offer more money. This is normally only a short-term fix for someone working outside of his or her talents. People either love the job (talent driven) or come for the money. Clock-watchers and paycheck employees aren't the best employees, and often the conditions were put in place by the business. This all sounds irrelevant in a book about executive coaching. So, let's punch it up a little.

Now for a more painful example: suppose the CEO makes a mistake with a high-powered, highly paid executive. Executives at this level, if they feel they have been wronged, tend to become litigious. They don't go quietly. Some will take your intellectual property or your clients with them. If you create a great culture, help your people find a career path in the firm, listen and help leaders get engaged, things generally go much better. If you don't, your legal expenses increase, as will your turnover; your reputation may be hurt, and you will need high-powered conflict resolutions systems at the ready.

One profession that is witnessing an exodus of

professionals is medicine, in particular, doctors. The paperwork keeps them from doing what they loved when they entered the medical profession. Findings from a 2014 study conducted by the Physicians Foundation (September 16, 2014, at http://www.physiciansfoundation.org/news/survey-of-20000-us-physicians-shows-80-of-doctors-are-over-extended-or-at):

- "Thirty-nine percent of physicians indicate that they will accelerate their retirement plans due to changes in the healthcare system
- Twenty-six percent of physicians now participate in an Accountable Care Organization (ACO), though only 13 percent believe ACOs will enhance quality and decrease costs
- Fifty percent of physicians indicate implementation of ICD-10 will cause severe administrative problems in their practices
- Physicians spend 20 percent of their time on non-clinical paperwork."

When Steve Jobs was alive, could you have imagined him quitting his position? If a position represents a near perfect talent fit, why would you want to stop? When do you expect Jeff Bezos to resign? I'm not sure Elon Musk is going to slow down. Apparently, Warren Buffett hasn't figured out that he is at the retirement age. It's pretty clear these people have enough money to kick back and retire. Why do they continue? They stay because they are having way too much fun doing what they love to do.

Burgeoning Bureaucracy

Too often when talents are not "front and center," the response of organizations is to increase the size of their workforce. The firm ends up becoming more process oriented and top-down in terms of structure and decision-making.

What appear to be gaps in an organization's business process is often a result of not fully using the strengths that exist in the organization. One soon finds out that people who don't have appropriate talent aren't very efficient and effective at their jobs. Consequently organizations hire people to fill talent and strength disparities. Imagine people working at 40 percent capacity in terms of their strengths rather than at 80 percent.

The more difficult problem occurs when you hire people who don't have enough to do. They create what is lovingly referred to as "make work." This manifests itself in things like excessive meetings. They create cumbersome new forms that become required, but that are not in fact needed. People begin building little kingdoms. It is absolutely true that more communication doesn't lead to better communication. Add that to technologies that are famous for miscommunicating. Email and messaging come to mind immediately. Can you honestly say you've never found yourself in a communication traffic jam caused by poorly worded emails? Sixty-five percent of communication is nonverbal. Save us from the emoji world we live in!

Bureaucratic divisional managers build their little kingdoms and often brag about how many people work for them. They might even be proud of how large their budgets are. Unfortunately the organization becomes more lethargic. Kingdom building represents a subtle way of saying, look how powerful I am. Ever notice how when companies are under financial duress, they can fire people even though they are able to provide similar levels of service despite the firings? When you add management layers, stand back and watch everything slow down. Inertia will rule the day.

Additionally, this is an extremely expensive proposition. When a firm adds a new layer of management, it doubles the work for those above and below that layer. In a growing firm, a better option is adding staff people rather than adding a new layer of management. The volume of work may be increasing, but having more decision makers slows down decision-making. As we add layers, the percentage of time spent in meetings will also become excessive; as a result, the work doesn't get done, so consequently even more people are hired. Time would be better spent working in teams. With the new layer of management, the larger, more risky decisions that would have been made quickly now languish for months or years before approval.

In summary, the overriding tendency is for organizations to bureaucratize as a way to rid themselves of weaknesses caused by misapplied talent. The misapplication of talent is complicated by an organization that consequently isn't responding to market changes; customer service often suffers; employee turnover increases; and customers vote with their feet.

Regrettably for taxpayers, the best example of bureaucratic overkill and misapplication of talent happens within the federal government and many state and local governmental units. As noted earlier, many governmental employees spend a fair amount of their nonproductive time talking about how many years they have before they can retire. Do such people sound like fully engaged employees? If the job fit was appropriate, why are people in government in such a hurry to retire?

Sadly organizational energy and resources are too often wasted in a feeble attempt at repairing human limitations. Such people problems are not insurmountable, but change begins with organizational commitment at the top, that is, commitment to hire and place people based on talent and, subsequently, developing talents into strengths for the betterment of the organization.

New Paradigm: The Strengths School of Management

The Strengths School of Management operates on the assumption that talent is God given or based on genetics, birth order, upbringing, and so forth. The central belief is that talent, much like temperament, doesn't dramatically change over time. It is further undergirded by positive psychology that focuses on putting strengths to work rather than focusing of repairing weaknesses.

Staffing for Strengths Leads to Success

There is an identifiable joy watching those who are fully engaged in their work. People intrinsically desire a sense of fulfillment in what they do. People are searching for meaning in their work. Individual identity is very much tied to what one does for a living. So engagement is the key issue to focus on even if an organization just wants its employees to be happier, say nothing of more productive.

There are significant spillover benefits for an organization when employees fully use their talents. One can witness CEOs saying, "No one could ever replace June." "I've never seen anyone as talented as Fred." "What Susan does is totally amazing."

Leaders with the appropriate talent and who are fully engaged will be in demand. Fully engaged people tend to have higher expectations. These workplace expectations can fall across a variety of fronts, including the desire for fun at work, allowing for relaxation when needed, creating access to tools and technology, initiating flexible hours, and so on. The opposite of engagement is disengagement, and it won't produce positive comments.

Additionally, there is a bottom-line financial benefit of having a fully engaged worker use his or her talent. Employees working their talents perform at higher levels and thus gain new organizational opportunities. This is essential for fast-growing companies. These firms fare better largely as a result of increasing productivity. If an organization doesn't reward recognizable talent, the competition soon will do so, consequently leading to voluntary exits and problematic turnover.

Time for an analogy: Why invest in a stock that doesn't provide at least some opportunity for high performance? Why focus energy and capital to convert talents into strengths, if not for the betterment of both the employee and the organization? Misusing talent is akin to an NFL quarterback being coached to take a position as a wide receiver. Can he catch the ball? Absolutely! But his gift is in strategy *and* passing the ball.

The following graph demonstrates the point.

Levels of Engagement and Consequential Behavior

0-40% Engagement	41-60% Engagement	61-80% Engagement	81-100% Engagement
The employee is likely to leave the organization or maybe stay but become a negative force in the workplace.	The employee is not likely to fully understand why she is not happy and effective.	This employee is likely to be hitting on all cylinders. He is enjoying his work. If engagement is near 80%, you as boss will like what you see.	This person is doing very well and everyone recognizes it. If the organization offers opportunity and provides a good working environment the fit is "near perfect" and will benefit both the employee and the organization.
The employee may become unsuccessful and, consequently, an excessive cost to manage. This is a misallocation of management time.	The employee is likely to be exploring options, putting out feelers, and looking into internal job postings in an honest attempt to secure a better position.	This employee is truly enjoying his job and is cautious about jumping into new opportunities unless they are a better fit for his talents.	Management is listening to this employee and doing everything possible to retain her.

I've previously recommended the StrengthsFinder for a CEO, but I also see it as one of the valuable tools for corporations/organizations to use in staffing and personnel development. Again, it is inexpensive, but the energy needed to make it valuable and profitable requires intentionality in terms of education, time, and use of human resources.

One danger when using StrengthsFinder (SF) is not going deep enough to ensure substantial understanding of potential applications. When used corporately, employees often take the assessment at a retreat; everyone enjoys the positive feedback. Then an executive might contact a Gallup Coach (full disclosure, I am one) and ask for a short program to debrief the assessed employees. The conversation goes something like this: "StrengthsFinder is easy to take, and we get it. We don't want to spend much money. We are pretty sure if you give us an hour, we can fully implement it." Wouldn't it be great if it were that easy?

- What about using SF to build amazing teams?
- What about using SF as one of the tools used in hiring?
- What about looking at job descriptions that force people to work outside of their talents? And making adjustments based on the findings?
- What about the bureaucratization of an organization because of misapplying talent?
- What about the damage we do by not making sure that we have gifted managers?
- What, if any, prospects do we have for building a fully engaged culture without first understanding and applying SF results?

Experienced coaches should refuse to take on these rather nonconsequential "debriefing" sessions. Why? They set the organization up for failure (and generally don't enhance the coach's reputation). Several days after the session, StrengthsFinder is a pleasant but inconsequential learning experience, and everyone gets back to "business as usual." It takes much more work to understand the value of the tool at a deeper level.

If the organization intends to improve its engagement, it will take a significant amount of work. A firm that desires the superior results will make the necessary commitments. For others, StrengthsFinder is nothing more than the "flavor of the month."

A good analogy is when one meets a person for the first time and is very excited and impressed but, as time goes on, fails to understand the person at a deeper, more significant level. Helping people to learn, fully understand, and then accurately apply StrengthsFinder is the key.

Once a StrengthsFinder plan is in place, the coach can help to implement what the organization needs from a business point of view, focusing on building a fully engaged strengths-based top management leadership team followed by a full implementation of teams for the entire work environment.

To secure success, StrengthsFinder content must become front and center, potentially discussed in all meetings. Minimally it should be referenced on a regular basis and used in determining who serves on various teams, committees, and so forth. All employees should list their top five talents on their business cards to help create the ever-present awareness needed to ensure success. Fortunately Gallup has created excellent tools that can be used to create fully engaged workplaces.

If a coach could achieve significant improvements in engagement, additional coaching could be built on that strong foundation. Much like a sports team, every player would be in the position that maximizes personal talents and coached to be the best in a key placement. Even if your organization does not use StrengthsFinder, a coach could be consciously and subconsciously thinking about how to employ talents and strengths to gain a significant organizational improvement.

Gallup coaches want to look at a leader's top ten talents (better yet, all thirty-four talents in order). The idea is that the top five represent the true person, and the second five are supporting (secondary). Dr. Donald O. Clifton, who spent a lifetime working on the Clifton StrengthsFinder, felt he could coach well by focusing only on the top two talents.

Gallup has proven that StrengthsFinder talents are relevant to everyone and every culture that has currently been researched. Many cultures have already employed the StrengthsFinder assessment with high levels of validity and reliability. StrengthsFinder 2.0 was one of the highest-selling books on Amazon during 2015. With the popularity of talent assessment, a common question is, now that I've taken StrengthsFinder, how can I begin working on my weaknesses?

StrengthsFinder is not intended to remove all weaknesses. The idea is to focus development on natural talent. If a weakness is so glaring that it is holding one back, then give some attention to it. But generally success will come from building on talent and strengths, rather than by spending inordinate amounts of time on eliminating weaknesses.

Many consider Dr. Clifton, who did the foundational research for StrengthsFinder, to be the father of positive psychology. I believe Peter Drucker deserves much of the credit for making the idea of building on strengths such a widely accepted concept. Additionally, strengths have defined biblical characters. The disciples each had strengths and weaknesses. Jesus began with flawed people who had legitimate strengths and who would with the power of the Holy Spirit and their talents change the world.

Assessing Managerial Strengths

Gallup has determined that only about 10 percent of managers have the correct talents to be managers. People often get promoted because they are good doers, but companies often don't do their homework to make sure the person being promoted has the talent to manage.

Nearly everyone has experienced both excellent and less than effective managers. Leaders often expect a person to fit a predetermined job description—with some measure of confidence based on the potential employee's previous performance. In their previous positions, such employees may well have been more fully engaged in their work. Question: will they be engaged in the new position? How would one know without a careful evaluation based on talent?

This may be the most common problem associated with promoting top-level people. Just because they were great doers doesn't mean they will be great managers. If I had a dollar for every time I faced this as a coach, I would already be retired.

What talents are essential to being a successful manager? Well, it partially depends on the requirements of the job. But the majority of companies get it wrong by creating criteria based on past performance, "Well, June was such a good doer; we thought she would be a great manager."

Gallup identifies five managerial "talent dimensions" (April 13, 2015, at http://www.gallup.com/businessjournal/182378/one-people-possess-talent-manage.aspx):

1. Motivator
2. Assertiveness
3. Accountability
4. Relationships
5. Decision-making

Obviously some analysis will need to be undertaken

to determine if a person is a good fit, but taking the time to get it right makes all the difference for the organization. If a poor decision is made, it will not be easy for the organization to fire the manager, and the misfit is not completely the newly hired manager's problem.

Flattening an Organization Promotes Engagement

CEOs who don't understand the importance of appropriately applying human talent are prone to hiring more managers, thus bureaucratizing their organizations. An additional danger is the CEO often compensates for misapplied talent by working ungodly hours. No wonder burnout is such a common CEO malady.

I argued for years that Microsoft was operating in too much of a monolithic manner. Now we see Microsoft attempting to return to the agility of her youth. GM has a similar problem further complicated by the high cost of her retirees. Sears, even though it has an iconic history, struggles with many layers of management and continues to fail. It may soon be on the chopping block. Take one huge, monolithic, ignorant organization and merge it with a similar organization, and from that you gain efficiency? I don't think so. Did communism, governed by a few bureaucrats at the top, perform better economically than its capitalistic adversaries? Or does capitalism with millions of individuals making decisions based on the price system work better? My thought is that the enormous size of an organization eventually becomes driven by the egos of those at the top and not by the desire for efficiency.

Coaching has allowed me (for several organizations) to assist in recalibrating managerial systems, with a goal of engagement, empowerment, and efficiency. In one organization, I had the privilege of working with Dr. John Maxwell, the now-famous leadership guru. I helped the leadership to create a program to eliminate middle management. (We turned middle managers into consultative advisors.) Top managers became the financial decision makers (operated as the bank). Each facility became a separate operating unit, built around a business plan, and managed by unit CEOs (basically local CEOs).

What we learned was fascinating. First, we could not predict which local CEOs would survive and prosper. Several of the local facility CEOs (working based on their talents) accomplished amazing results. Others who we thought would be effective (based on what we learned while working in the previous organization) only looked effective because their supervisors had been excellent. Many were not prepared to lead or knowledgeable about their talents, and they failed.

Our initial plan called for a three- to five-year layered implementation process. The CEO decided he wanted to quicken the pace, flipping model for implementation within a year. We asked Dr. Maxwell how many local CEOs we would lose, and he said 70 to 80 percent. He was spot on. Too much change, too fast, and not enough time to analyze the cards we were holding.

Overall, the reorganization was very successful, but many local CEOs quickly prospered and many quickly failed. As noted above, the CEO of the organization sped up the proposed changes, thus limiting the success only to those who could quickly adapt and prosper. I believed the leaders with the appropriate talents and temperaments were the winners.

Again, Gallup's research has shown that only 10 percent of managers are naturally talented to be managers. I wish we would have known that prior to or during our reorganization. Oddly enough, the successful managers at this organization represented roughly the same percentages that Gallup research now validates (March 25, 2014, at http://www.gallup.com/businessjournal/167975/why-great-managers-rare.aspx).

How about Your Organization—Behavioral School or Strengths School?

Do you attempt to change people or build on their natural talents and strengths? A good coach will be pushing a CEO to thoroughly evaluate this question. Depending on how the question is answered, the positive or negative consequences for the organization are enormous. It is possible that an organization sees tremendous success by simply going through this process and/or refocusing based on talent.

The refocusing process is why an executive coach desires to work directly with the CEO. If the CEO is not on board, the process will fail. If it is impossible to gain the support of the CEO, the coach will likely be relegated to helping the CEO with some of the short-term issues (as listed) in chapter 11. If that happened, an excellent coach will still be worth the price paid. Keep in mind the focus of this book is crushing the CEO's paradigm. That is why the CEO must see how changing her or his paradigm is the logical starting point.

If you decide to build a strengths-based organization, consider having a team or a steering committee composed of people at different levels of the organization. Let employees begin looking at their talents and think about teams (see chapter 7) and how to divide the work based on talents and strengths.

A workforce developed on a strengths-based structure is best executed with a team approach. Give the teams the ability to operate independently. Let them manage their resources and deal with internal problems. Clearly communicate that they are accountable for results. Remind them that results only happen outside the organization, in the marketplace. If employees buy in, the result will be very good.

Most people who are fully engaged in their jobs do not realize how much the job defines them. Money is important, but it is not enough to produce fulfillment at work. Everyone needs to find meaning in life.

Working outside of one's talent will lead to an unhappy work life. In such cases, many don't "truly live" until they retire. Some never do find their path and thus spend their twilight years trying to find meaning in their play. Many just wear out the remote on their televisions. It's never too late to learn about your talent. A purposeful life should be the goal. The book *The Purpose-Driven Life* was a huge success because it hit a nerve. People want to do work that encompasses meaning. It is also doing what is enjoyable—based on operative talents.

Chapter 6

Values and Corporate Culture: Get It Right

Working with an executive coach, a board or CEO can identify and hone (1) personal and corporate values and (2) a corporate culture with the goal of maximizing stakeholder engagement, efficiency, and profitability. Let's first look at personal and corporate values.

Personal Values That Define Your "Brand"

How do you think your employees perceive you? If we asked your employees to list your values, do you think your list would match theirs? Maybe you'd think in terms of your image, which is based on superficial realities. For example, image might indicate that a leader drives the "right kind of car." He wears the right kind of suit. Her office is on the top floor. His watch is a Rolex. A person can easily improve the image by hiring an image consultant and taking the advice given.

I prefer to think in terms of branding, which confirms or reflects the concrete (long-term) essence of a person. Image plays a role, but it is secondary to branding. I worked for an organization that was led by someone who seemed to be the most frugal CEO on earth. Although the organization benefited financially, employees felt diminished because money was always more important than people. The CEO also was a "convenient forgetter." Verbal promises about significant issues were made and easily dispensed with by saying, "I forgot." When confronted by an employee, it was clear that forgetfulness was not based on honest memory loss, but rather on his need for extreme frugality. This was not a good example of positive branding.

A positive brand has the power to move people. It is based on performance and is experienced in reality. The substance of a person is demonstrated by the impact she has on colleagues. Therefore, the real person is on display every day in the workplace. The brand is relatively long-term, predictable, and dependable. Image, not so much.

For example, Ronald Reagan had the reputation of being an excellent communicator, but what was most compelling was his demonstrative love of people. The Federal Reserve increased interest rates in the early 1980s. Interest rates were extremely high, and the unemployment rate went above 10 percent. At one point Reagan stayed the course, while virtually everyone wanted him to back out of his inflation-reduction plan. He was actually sending personal checks to people who were in trouble. He didn't do it for the branding. What he did came from his heart. Powerful branding!

Sam Donaldson, the now-retired ABC News correspondent, said he disagreed with Reagan on nearly everything but liked him personally. Likability is hard to fake. Ron Jr., when speaking at his mother's funeral, said, "My dad felt that man was 'basically good.'" He trusted people implicitly. Nancy was there to verify—to sense whether the president's feelings were justified.

So whereas image is superficial, branding is not. What proceeds from the mouth of a CEO tells everyone a great deal about the CEO. Oral and written communication is crucial and reflects the brand. The talents of a CEO that are at work in the organization speak volumes.

Branding creates expectations that normally play out in a fairly consistent fashion. This is true for products, services, and for people. For example, at our local shopping mall one night, my wife and I ordered Chick-fil-A. When I got my sandwich, it was cold. Shocked, I looked at the sandwich and said (out loud), "Oh, no." People around me wondered what was up. Thankfully, it has never again happened to me at a Chick-fil-A. Branding is a guide that creates expectations. Chick-fil-A rarely fails, and their sandwiches are normally perfect.

The 2016 presidential political election, with few exceptions, indicated that rebranding could have helped both candidates. This seemed to be deeper than image; the heart and the integrity of the candidates were found to be revealing. The negative detours taken by candidates on both sides indicated that the desire for power was greater than the respect they had for the office of the presidency. Many citizens didn't feel that either candidate understood what the populace was about. Many wonder, could these people have benefited from heeding a strong coach?

The core of the CEO is the CEO's values, and those values provide the foundation for the organization's values. The CEO's values create a culture that defines what is important and how things get done. Likewise the picture created by the organization is a good representation of the

CEO.

I was a coach and consulted for a regional construction company. With a "value's exercise," we discovered that some fifty employees listed virtually the same top twenty corporate values. The employees were living out their corporate worldview. Values are the glue that holds the organization together. Such a solid organization would be able to weather about anything including an empowerment intervention process.

At a separate construction company, we followed the same exercise and there was no agreement as to values. So I asked the employees the following questions:

- Is your company ethical? Answer: not so much.
- Does your company feel involvement in the community is important? Answer: not so much.
- Does the company pay its bills on time? Answer: not really.
- Does the company provide career opportunities for its employees? Answer: no.

And so the questions continued. After pressing harder, we determined there was one value perceived to be important to the CEO. The value was "volume." "We do a lot of foundations." This is not much of a positive endorsement. So I'm wondering, would you want to hire this firm?

How do you feel your organization would do in the

same exercise?

CEOs are going to live out their values, and their personal branding will create an organizational culture. Is your branding positive? What do people feel when you enter the room? A positive culture experiences less employee turnover—especially of people in leadership positions.

People want to operate based on a system of right and wrong. It is interesting to me that when someone says, "there are no absolutes," they are assuming what they say is absolute. As CEOs help determine what is right and wrong in the organization, they are creating a foundation for their culture.

The coach's role is to help strengthen positive values and minimize negative values. What do I see as the most compelling values? Integrity, honesty, stewardship, and the value of others are my favorites. It's hard to work in a world without these values.

The goal for a coach is to help the CEO create a positive corporate environment—thus improving the brand.

A Two-Way Street

I haven't yet used the word *ethics*, but on one level that's what I'm talking about. Research has consistently shown that a CEO's ethics impact the entire leadership team. Ethical CEOs end up having more ethical top managers, and unethical CEOs tend to breed unethical top managers.

Adam Smith, the father of free-market capitalism, believed the primary ethical control mechanism in capitalism was the community. In other words, if you were unethical, the entire community would know it and share the news. Of course, a large city may allow a company to dodge ethics for a period of time simply by finding new clients who hadn't learned about the firm's past.

So apply the Adam Smith analogy to an organization: CEOs benefit by having someone at every level in the organization who will tell the truth about how it feels to work at that level. People at various levels can reveal the worldview and ethics of the organization as they see it. A CEO who is approachable and transparent will find that these relationships are easy to develop. In summary, the clearest understanding comes when one gains perfect honesty from others.

The television program *Undercover Boss* demonstrates the point very well. And it is true that you can't always walk a mile in another's shoes, but positive interpersonal communication can illuminate and ultimately change the thinking of a CEO. In this way, corporate ethics can become a two-way street.

Corporate Culture 101

It would be no surprise for me to say that every corporation or organization has a "culture." Whether acknowledged or unspoken, there's a "this is the way things here get done" and a corresponding "why." Terrence Deal and Allan

Kennedy, in their classic 1982 book *Corporate Cultures: The Rites and Rituals of Corporate Life*, provide the basics for understanding culture.

A founder might have set the culture in motion. If the organization is young, the founder's values and mode might still prevail. Sometimes whole societal segments seem to share a common culture. I think of higher education. Universities are known for adding layers of management when all that is needed is additional support people. Consequently they have trouble taking innovations to the marketplace. They become intensely process oriented. Their decision-making becomes constipated. Personal example: At one point the university where I was employed had nine or more layers of management. Their organizational chart was unintelligible.

Once "process organizations" realize they have created a less-than-beneficial financial milieu, they may bring in a new CEO, who will reduce the bureaucratic layers and sharpen business processes. The change will be quite threatening to those who were comfortable in the aforementioned "process culture."

Highly educated people tend to favor adding structure to solve problems. CEOs in "process cultures" learn that more structure allows them to redistribute the blame for problems to others. In the end, job security becomes a high value in financially strapped process organizations.

Even within organizational functions, every institution has a culture, influenced or set in motion by a

CEO. When a board hires a CEO—or a CEO hires subordinate executives—a foundational question should be, is the new executive a "culture fit"?

Executives coming from a very different corporate culture may struggle to adjust to new values and new processes. Those who hire a CEO should be looking for the culture fit, as well as the values fit, and the suitability of a candidate given related organizational issues.

Conversely, maybe a CEO was hired to radically change the culture. Rarely can a culture be comprehensively changed in the short run. Normally a CEO finds the positive elements in the organization and attempts to multiply their impact in the broader organization. Only in an emergency is it possible to change a culture in a short period of time. In an emergency (failing organization) there is no other option.

I worked for a company in the business of acquiring decertified nursing homes. It was not unusual for a poorly managed nursing home to be on the precipice of failure. The new CEO would show up, lay down the law, and expect major change quickly. Often a rather relaxed facility in terms of management style would be facing a dramatic change in culture. The local managers were given specific mandates that had to be achieved in a week. If they were not, their jobs were on the line.

An example of negative change can happen when two organizations are merged with no prior plan—the CEO just announces the merger and lets the new organization work it out the problems. One such company (that I consulted for) ended up with two vice presidents in nearly every function. In such a organization, you might find two vice presidents in marketing wondering who would be the last person standing the next day. In the short-run, this amounts to a disaster; the casualties will include some of the best people. But change doesn't have to be this chaotic and traumatic.

Corporate Values

We briefly considered the personal values of leaders. What about values of companies, especially in terms of customers? And then employees—those who are thriving and those who are floundering?

Corporate Values and Customers

I love the book *How Full Is Your Bucket?* by Tom Rath, but I take exception to his advice, to "do unto others as they would have you do unto them." Be careful about reversing the Golden Rule. The Golden Rule assumes that your values are positive and not negotiable.

Rath might not take his idea that far, but businesses should run on a clear, positive, set of ethical values that are admired by outsiders. I would have stated Rath's idea this way: do unto others as they would have them do under them providing you don't compromise your values on the way. There are certain things you might want that I am unwilling to give; I won't give away the store or compromise my values. For example, I won't sell you unethical or potentially harmful products, even if you want them.

Always be careful when someone proposes a change to your corporate values, mission, and vision. Understand, in a comprehensive way, how such changes will play out in reality. Politics provides many examples of giving others what they want only to see it dramatically damage the United States.

Some corporate value choices might need to be thoroughly discussed. For example, GM might want to reconsider depending too much on the lowest bidder. Apple might want to consider what impact Chinese sweatshops will have on its pristine image. Politicians might want to revisit "expectation theory": what you promise to me, I will expect you to deliver.

Corporate Values and Employees

Companies that possess positive values will often help a failing executive, and thus make helpful adjustments to facilitate a soft landing for the executive at a new organization. If an ineffectively performing executive is unlucky enough to work for an organization with negative values (coupled with the inability to understand talent and strengths), the executive's tenure may be short-lived. Additionally, the executive may be stigmatized in the broader industry he or she serves in, raising roadblocks to securing a new position. The scenario might look like this:

	Ethical/Positive Corporate Values	Unethical/Negative Corporate Values
Employee Strengths Mismatch	The employee suffers, but the organization's positive approach minimizes the pain. The organization may see its error and adjust the job, thus rebuilding a relationship with the employee or at minimum helping the employee find a soft landing elsewhere.	In this scenario, the employee and the organization both are likely to suffer. Additionally, the organization may not be helpful in aiding the employee land a better position elsewhere. The employee will be facing a tough job search, burdened with past performance that is difficult to explain.

Alternatively, suppose an executive gains a position at a less-than-ethical organization, but is allowed to use his or her strengths. If the firm doesn't recognize the talent, a competitor will likely see the executive excelling and will hire her away. An excellent outcome for the employee, but it is not so great for the organization.

	Ethical/Positive Corporate Values	Unethical/Negative Corporate Values
Employee Strengths	Employee longevity on the job is likely to result in both the	The employee is subject to the organization's short-term thinking. The

Match	organization and the employee prospering. The employee establishes an excellent record of accomplishment.	organization suffers. The employee, although happy with the content of the job, likely works to secure a better job at a positive competitor that appreciates proven success.

Corporate Values and Culture: Getting It Right Is Imperative

A CEO engages and leads his or her workplace in terms of its culture and values. Deal and Kennedy created a matrix that simplistically demonstrates four corporate cultures

	Quick Feedback	**Slow Feedback**
High Risk	Tough-Guy, Macho	Bet-Your-Organization
Low Risk	Work Hard, Play Hard	Process

Let's look at these one at a time.

Tough-Guy, Macho Culture

People who flourish in this culture have an ability to deal with very challenging situations that involve a high level of risk and quick feedback. Entrepreneurs fit well into this framework, as do brain surgeons. There is not much time to adjust and not many ways to adequately control risk in tough-guy, macho situations.

National cultures throughout the world where leaders worry about "losing face" have a difficult time competing against national cultures where risk taking is welcomed and even celebrated. For example, China is known for its ability to replicate great products, but not very adept at creating new innovations. The United States excels when it comes to innovation.

Bet-Your-Organization/Company Culture

This culture involves high risk but slow feedback. An example would be the process of building a new military weapon system or a sophisticated breakthrough technology. The stakes are high, and one may not know for years whether the products will actually work. Currently SpaceX is making huge investments in space travel; what keeps the high-risk and slow-feedback process going is the intensity of the entrepreneur at the top, Elon Musk. Musk proves that superior vision and intensity can move the bet-your-organization culture forward quickly almost to the point where it might be defined as a tough-guy, macho culture.

Work Hard/Play Hard Culture

This involves low risk and fast feedback, exemplified by a sales-oriented culture. This culture is exceedingly competitive, where leaders are acutely aware of their competitors even in their own workplace. For example, some organizations post an individual's sales results on the wall to create an intensely competitive environment where no one sale or event sinks the organization, but the competitive environment drives short-term results. This culture often is very intense, but also playful.

Process Culture

In this culture, feedback is slow, and the risks are low. The best example is likely to be government. The wheels of progress move slowly. Large companies, institutions of higher education, and public utilities are excellent examples. Every decision in a process culture revolves around the process. A common question is, did the decision go through the appropriate committees? If one thrives in a tough-guy, macho culture, working in a process culture might drive him insane.

Best Fit?

What culture is the best fit for a new hire? The organization may not know how to answer that question. Many companies have components of each culture, but the driving question is, what is the overall cultural context? A bad fit can lead to low employee engagement.

For example, as a young man I worked for Prudential, a very structured and process-driven company. Insurance companies, with their marble buildings and manicured grounds, send a message of permanence and dependability. Everything moved slowly. We often talked about being owned by "Mother Pru." The starting pay was marginal, but the benefits were wonderful. If you were a process person, you would love the safe feeling. Prudential proudly stated, "We never laid anyone off during the Great Depression." Wow. If you were a process-culture person, no greater words could ever have been spoken. Even the name indicated that in all things "great care would be taken." The promise was to be prudent.

Frankly, I was bored out of my mind. Prudential is an excellent company, but I was made for a work hard/play hard or a tough-guy, macho culture.

To further complicate the culture question, many organizational leaders build strategic plans that their culture will never be able to implement effectively. For example, it is not unusual for people in process cultures to plan for huge shifts in new-product development. Such companies will typically be moving very slowly while the tough guy, macho organizations successfully build the innovation more quickly and effectively.

When hiring, key strategic questions can single out a candidate's culture-fit fairly quickly. (Having said that, I emphasize that Peter Drucker notes that all decisions could be made expeditiously except for hiring decisions. Take your time when hiring.) For example, if an organization is proposing an innovation that would be best handled by a tough-guy, macho culture-type, an interviewer might ask an applicant, "We are wanting to take a product nationally. Please indicate where you have done that in the past." Or, "Currently how long does it take your organization to take a new product to the market?"

If the innovation requires high risk and slow feedback (as seen in a bet-your-organization culture), one might ask, "Tell me about your past successes at creating complex, long-term experimental innovations." Or, "In the past, what is the most capital your firm has raised for a major project?" "How close did your results align with your long-term pro forma projections?" "Was your project successful, or did the competition beat you to the market?"

In a process culture, you might ask, "Tell us about your ability to gain agreement when working through a complex decision-making framework." Or, "Tell us about your ability to get many competing interests to buy into a newly proposed program." Or, "How many layers of management does your organization have?" One frustration in politics is that nothing ever happens quickly, and the cost of administration is staggering.

Deal and Kennedy wrote their first comprehensive book on the subject (*Corporate Cultures*) in 1982 and updated it in 2000. The staying power of their work demonstrates the power of both their research and ideas. Many other books on corporate culture have followed, but

Deal and Kennedy's work is the best place to begin. I highly recommend Deal and Kennedy's work.

Financial Resources and Corporate Culture

One of the most significant determiners of culture is how the organization deals with money. For example, one might ask, what is more important, people or money? What is the organization's role in helping the larger community? How is conflict handled (money is often an important ingredient in resolving conflict)? How often has the organization taken a major risk that could have ended in financial disaster? How litigious is the company in protecting its interests?

Many companies take big risks in the early years but become more process oriented over time. Think about the fledgling baby Microsoft versus Microsoft now. Think about Apple in the early years following Steve Jobs' return versus now. It is easy to see that continuous risk taking is unusual behavior.

One key focus for coaching is helping organizations deal with conflict. Numerous conflict resolution methods have been developed. A coach will begin by exploring the underlying reasons why conflict becomes a problem for an organization. Don't be surprised if financial resources play a significant role. This is true, even at home. It is sometimes either dad's new boat or mom's new living room furniture— not both.

Typical solutions involve conciliation processes, including arbitration, but unfortunately lawsuits often become the final resort. After interviewing ten CEOs, I wrote a paper and delivered a presentation at the Saïd Business School at Oxford University in November 2015. Nearly all of these CEOs had created resolution systems for reoccurring conflicts. These were initiated to reduce the costs associated with conflict resolution.

The most common reason for major organizational conflict was new software implementations. Leadership got blamed for not doing a better job of researching the ramifications of new software. Information technology got blamed for not being prepared. The ripples were felt throughout the organization. Notable resources were spent in a desire to get the implementation right. In my research, it was determined that most conflict could have been eliminated had the organization spent more time planning for what to do when things failed to work out as intended.

It is difficult to defuse a bomb once it has gone off. Thus preempting major conflicts before they take place is critical. As noted, conflict resolution is very expensive for organizations, but the damage done to the overall organization is even more expensive. How conflict is dealt with has a huge impact on the organizational culture. Take, for example, the influence of informal internal channels of communication. Conflict provides a good amount of negative theater for employees and customers to consume. This is where a coach can play a key role in minimizing some of the negative internal and external impact as well as helping the leadership develop preemptive methods to stop conflict before it happens.

In hiring a coach, a CEO should consider choosing

someone who has been heavily involved in dealing with corporate change, reorganization, and conflict resolution. A coach's personal involvement with such changes will be more valuable than all the books written about corporate culture.

Company Culture and Conflict

It is surprising how many CEOs fail to deal with conflict until there is a lawsuit initiated by an employee. This is problematic since the CEO is responsible for both preserving and growing financial resources. In our increasingly litigious country, we see many frivolous employee-driven lawsuits: yet, many organizations can preempt lawsuits by showing concern for employee issues.

The vast majority of potential conflicts are resolved when organizations create mechanisms for dealing with conflict. One of the easiest involves a simple fact-finding process. It begins with a process managed by the two combatants each picking three people who they believe are trustworthy. These people gather facts relating to the relevant conflict. Subsequently, the parties evaluate the facts. Once the facts are laid out, most conflicts are ended. As a result, a large company will see a major reduction in lawsuits.

In a sense, this was a conciliation process. Such a process requires organizational openness, transparency, and a willingness to work through issues. This clearly is not rocket science, but an executive coach can help a CEO find a path for reducing conflict, not only to save the organization money, but also to facilitate the development of a healthier corporate culture.

Culture Recap

Often people don't work effectively in corporate cultures that are not a fit. A CEO needs to understand the type of culture each employee will be most productive in. It would difficult to understand what culture to place a new employee in unless the CEO understands his or her own culture. Deal and Kennedy's model is a good starting point, but it would be helpful if the CEO could list the corporate values and then describe the culture. Next, it would be helpful to ask the employees about what they think the corporate values are. Does the CEO's perception of values match what the employees see as the "values" that are operative in the firm? Once everyone is clear about the values and culture, it should be part of the conversation when hiring new people, especially potential leaders.

Chapter 7

Team Engagement

- Would you know how to ensure a team has the best members and the greatest chances for success?
- Would you know how to create a development process for those team members who are not adequately using their talents, thus helping them convert talents into strengths?

In an earlier chapter, I discouraged the excessive use of individual job descriptions, deeming them counterproductive. Thankfully teams have emerged as a dominant structural approach, thus making job descriptions much less important in terms of hiring and evaluation.

If human resource people begin to think about the variety of talents, strengths, and experiences that will be needed in a position, they will be ready to look for applicants. Then an incoming employee needs to be evaluated. This involves CEOs thinking about employees, their talents and proven strengths along with how they might contribute to an organization's internal environment. One thing that would help employees thrive is focusing on organizational empowerment.

Empowerment occasionally has been the subject of

scorn. Some leaders feel that empowerment was built by hippies for free-spirited people. The concept of empowerment has endured because now organizations are attempting to manage what Peter Drucker foresaw and named "knowledge workers." How does one put that idea into a job description? Even thinking of a strong analogy to describe "knowledge workers" seems to fall short.

Empowered organizations make sure employees have the freedom to work based on their talents; in the past two decades the technology sector of the economy has led the way in creating such environments. Millennial employees seem to operate best in organizations that allow for a more free-flowing, goal-oriented workplace. These young people have some lofty expectations, but carefully working with them and employing systems such as open management, flex-scheduling, goal-oriented work environment and teams will allow CEOs to hire, train, retain, and harvest their talent—as they work together in teams.

Members of a healthy team have one thing in common: they're able to focus on the requisite talent each team member brings to the table. Team members see the strengths of teammates emerge. How might this impact the use of strict personal job descriptions?

Occasionally I've seen team members take each of their individual job descriptions and identify how the accumulated talent pool of the team can be reallocated to facilitate a better application of talent for the team. Occasionally the human resource personnel will write a job description that identifies perfectly what the team is to do. Then a team itself might start the process of determining who can best handle each job description sub-definition.

If neither method is employed, the team will, in time, begin to work through the process, given the traditional team-building sequence of forming, storming, norming, and performing. Let's say the team is working with a coach. The coach's goal is to speed up the team-building process in an attempt to quickly facilitate team effectiveness. The team-leader position requirements can be quite broad. The finest teams seem to understand rather quickly how they can multiply the impact of the team leader.

Engagement Speeds Up Team Effectiveness

Teams need time to develop. Ever hear an NFL coach talk about the rebuilding process? Time allows team members to see what each team member's talents are, thus allowing the team to test out those skills. Over time, team members start leaning on the strengths of others in the team. In about twelve to fourteen weeks, the team will be on the road, so to speak.

Watching a team that has worked together for a significant amount of time can be a beautiful sight. For example, watching a framing crew (with team longevity) frame up a house is true art. Even a healthy family can demonstrate team effectiveness when every family member both understands and can perform the assigned responsibility.

Teams that have to deal with more complexity and divergent projects will need additional time to jell. Excellent coaches work to motivate individual team members to employ their talents. When the team starts to click, performance will kick into high gear.

So given enough time, a team will begin to work based on its talent and strengths but will often need help to perceive what talent is needed but absent. For example, if a team doesn't have any (in StrengthsFinder terminology) executing talents, things won't get done in an expeditious way. If the team lacks influencing talents, it will take longer for the team to have the broad impact. If the team is missing relationship-building talents, team cohesiveness suffers. If the team lacks strategic thinking, the team's focus might be too "now" oriented and not sufficiently future oriented.

A Mix of Temperaments Leads to Well-Rounded Teams

Temperament is our tendency to react in certain predictable ways to given situations. One of several Merriam-Webster definitions for *temperament* is "characteristic or habitual inclination or mode of emotional response." Inscape Publishing has a tremendous tool called the DISC profile. This assessment tool can provide information about how individuals tend to react in different situations. It is very much like the Myers-Briggs Type system, but (in my opinion) has better applications for business.

Temperament is another strong indicator of what career path a person will enjoy. A rule of thumb in business is that employees need to love 60 percent or more of what they do and dislike only 40 percent or less. Leaders would like this percentage to soar higher than 60, but when it goes lower, there will be recognizable dissatisfaction. Once dissatisfaction becomes overwhelming, the person will often leave the job or simply be unhappy and unproductive. The basic DISC temperaments include:

Dominance (basic characteristics):

1. Impatience
2. High ego strength
3. Enjoys and even promotes change
4. Motivated by: directness and bottom-line results
5. Fears: personal criticism and people not keeping their commitments

Influencing (basic characteristics):

1. Emotional
2. Talkative
3. Not particularly good with detail
4. Motivated by: friendship
5. Fears: not being appreciated, not getting the limelight

Steadiness (basic characteristics):

1. Loyalty
2. Dislikes change

3. Detail-oriented
4. Motivated by: traditional practices and routine work
5. Fears: loss of stability

Conscientiousness (basic characteristics):

1. Logical
2. Intuitive
3. Perfectionistic
4. Motivated by: the "right way" to do things
5. Fears: personal criticism

The good news is that the vast majority of people are a mix of temperaments. Building on one's strengths and minimizing one's limitations is the key.

A team that exhibits a variety of temperaments will more likely "secure success" quickly. Imagine the infighting if a team is made up of dominant people where everyone wants to be in charge. A team full of conscientious temperaments, driven by individualization, would exhibit everyone working on her own plan rather than working together. "Steadiness" people like tradition and don't want to be in charge. In such a group, progress would not come quickly. "Influencing" people are socializers and can waste time if not held to timeframes. Bottom-line: teams require a variety of temperament and a mix of talent.

Team Relationships and Roles Are Important

Donald Phillips, author of *Run to Win: Vince Lombardi on Coaching and Leadership*, notes that in Vince Lombardi's day, "Teamwork was the key to the Green Bay Packers success. They didn't perform simply for individual glory. They did it because they loved one another."

As a teacher and trainer, I have learned one important thing about productive teams. They are most effective when team leaders understand how to be successful. Success is secured when the team leader clearly understands what others in the team bring to the process. Goals will drive the process. Effective team leaders teach fellow team members to lean into and consequently use the talents of other team members.

A Dramatic Example of Team Engagement

A few years back, when I was observing a major class project—students working with a real firm—the value of teamwork was dramatically portrayed. One strategic marketing team comprised four members. The team leader was remarkably talented; one other team member, although reserved, was a jewel in the rough. Two other members had never demonstrated any real engagement in their learning nor had they ever displayed their true talents and abilities.

The team was working with a telecom/tech organization, applying diffusion theory (product adoption theory) to the products and services provided by the company. When the team presented the final product, I did something I had never done before in the classroom. I stopped the class, and said, "It is unusual to single out a team for superior performance, especially with everyone else present, but this is one of the finest projects I have ever witnessed in the classroom. I believe this is Harvard Business School material."

Roughly four years later, I asked the previous team leader to update the project for presentation at Harvard. The paper was accepted, and I presented the research at the International Journal of Arts and Sciences Conference in May 2013.

One college student was able to see, develop, and employ the strengths of her team, and the outcome was exceptional. Her number-1 talent was Woo (winning others over). Team members loved her, loved working together, loved her ability to help them focus on the high standards, and loved putting their strengths to work.

With solid teams, $2 + 2$ rarely equals 4. It always equals much more. Talent employed by a gifted individual often is the spark, but noteworthy accomplishments are created by the input of a healthy team via significant contributions from all team members.

The Role of an Awesome Team Leader

Team leaders reflect many of the talents needed by managers.

Certainly the five areas mentioned earlier (the five

Gallup talent dimensions for managers) are important for team leaders. As a motivator, a team leader has to gain support and engage high-performing as well as lower-performing team members. The idea is that every team member is motivated to perform at the highest level possible.

Occasionally a team leader has to be assertive to keep the team moving and to manage internal team conflict. Unresolved problems don't go away. The team leader must take his or her share of the responsibility for problems and be open to input, thereby creating an atmosphere of transparency for all team members.

Accountability comes from setting and holding team members accountable for achieving goals. Various teaching techniques can engender engagement and motivation, by celebrating successes and honestly discussing areas where the team or team member can do better. One helpful visual method is to have regularly scheduled accomplishment meetings, say monthly or bimonthly. At these meetings, the team leader has each member write his or her goals on the board, followed by highlighting successes in green and failures in red. Soon team members will not want to be writing anything in red. The team leader can suggest ways for each team member to help facilitate the success of colleagues. Remember to celebrate the big wins!

Positive relationships are essential. Decision-making is pivotal if the team is going to perform at or above expectations. The team leader must clarify how decision-making works. For example, is the leader going to make the decision? Is the team gathering information to come alongside the leader in making a decision? Is the decision going to be democratic in nature, that is, every team member gets a vote? Clarity is essential in this regard.

What else is needed? Often the team leader is responsible for breaking down barriers with the larger organization. A team leader may be expected to secure additional resources. The team leader wears many hats, but the most endearing quality is to advocate for and recognize the accomplishments of the full team as well as individual team members.

As an aside, the use of interdisciplinary teams is gaining in popularity during the past couple of decades. Interdisciplinary teams are most helpful when the company is developing a new product or a new service. A recent BBC report noted that more than two hours on social media actually makes people lonelier, may cause envy as we look at other people's lives, and may create feelings of exclusion. When social media came into existence, perhaps interdisciplinary teams that included social and psychological researchers would have revealed such possible outcomes ("US Psychologists Claim Social Media 'Increases Loneliness,'" BBC Newsbeat, March 6, 2017 at https://apple.news/AIu8Mf5zyTj-QzZW2hN-scw).

Much of the recent (noteworthy) work in reference to new product development via interdisciplinary teams has happened with David Kelly and his Silicon Valley firm IDEO. Kelley also founded Stanford University's Hasso Plattner Institute of Design, known as the d.school. A great example of design thinking and collaboration is demonstrated in this TED video *How to Build Your Creative Confidence* (March 2012, at https://www.ted.com/talks/david_kelley_how_to_build_your

_creative_confidence).

Multiple perspectives take us beyond cross-functional thinking and are helpful in determining what customers will find useful.

Finally, intra-team health can be enhanced by understanding and using a concept called, "the emotional bank." Every team member must take each opportunity to make a deposit in the emotional bank of all other team members. Going the extra mile (emotionally) by demonstrating a desire to put others first sets you up for receiving a positive return/withdrawal when you need forgiveness for a mistake. If a fellow team member is already upset with you, an additional problem will make it difficult for that person to give you extra grace. Team problems are likely to be forgiven quickly if each team member's emotional bank is running over. See *How Full Is Your Bucket?* by Tom Rath.

Chapter 8

Communication Confidence

So where does wisdom come from? The book of Proverbs states (in a variety of ways, more than twenty times) that a wise person seeks counsel. As I've said in previous chapters, a coach brings a new perspective, a new approach, and a new attitude that can help ensure success in recalibrating an organization. Outsiders often bring a new perspective, and they certainly are not captives of the organization. There's an old joke that says a consultant/coach will likely be taken seriously—if he or she lives more than fifty miles away. Responding to critics, Jesus himself said, "A prophet is not without honour, but in his own country, and among his own kin, and in his own house." KJV (Mark 6:4). Sounds a bit like the fifty-mile rule.

For better or for worse, outsiders are taken more seriously because they are not captives of the company. Building effective organizations more often than not requires outside accountability, coupled with up-to-date intervention tools. Hiring a coach, you'll want to make sure the outsider has the experience, the knowledge, and the wisdom to infuse the organization with new ideas.

The coach will need a winsome attitude and a natural ability to connect with people. A purely analytical personality will likely not be accepted. This is unfortunate because the analytic person may be the smartest—but may lack the social skills to convince the leadership to change.

Employee buy-in is what makes the process work.

An Excellent Method for Refocusing Organizational Talent

The focus of this chapter is on the facilitation of excellent communication, but before we get there, let's recap/summarize an excellent method for refocusing organizational talent.

1. First, the executive coach works to gain top management support for focusing on talent. The executive coach ends up doing coaching that is often mixed with some consulting in order to achieve results. If top management doesn't regard focusing on talent as important, it won't happen. That is why coaches start with the CEO and those at the top of the firm. Coaching will advance the professional growth of the leaders (specifically the CEO), and everyone in the organization will profit as well by the growth that logically results from having more effective leaders.

2. Next, the coach will want to determine individual talent and strengths that reside in the firm. Discovering talent and subsequently looking for ways to harvest the talent is key. Latent talent must be unlocked and used as well.

3. Find and develop excellent managers and team leaders. Great managers are the heart of a successful business process, and they drive the bottom-line results. Making sure managers have the tools and training they need is essential.

4. Work on engagement. The coach will want to get people working on their talents and thus converting talent into strengths. Subsequently, the coach will work to help the organization develop an engaging culture that both recognizes and employs talent. Gallup has some amazing tools for assessing and consequently implementing these kinds of changes.

5. Facilitate building high-powered teams where 2 + 2 equals something more than 4—where teams can be more efficient than the functional or structural frameworks that are currently in place.

6. Focus on mission, vision, and values that set a foundation for building an engaging organization. The employer/employee relationship is a co-branding event essential for organizational success. Employees want to be proud of where they work, at an organization that is ethical, competent, and on the cutting edge.

7. Work on structural issues that are counterproductive to developing a positive, engaging workplace. Bureaucracy is a killer, so coaches will help CEOs take a careful look at how to reduce red tape and increase productivity.

8. Encourage the individual strength-building process that continues to move the organization in the direction of positive economic outcomes. A prosperous and growing organization will create new opportunities for both current and future employees.

9. Work toward a flatter, more robust organization that will make talent and leadership easy to recognize. Superior organizations understand that this is imperative.

10. Encourage employees to think like owners, rather than order-takers. Each employee needs a level of global understanding, that is, knowing how the firm makes money (or secures surpluses, in the case of a nonprofit) and creates new opportunities.

11. Work on branding to get customers engaged. What can the firm learn from the customers? How can you creatively move forward to build what customers will want next?

12. Good news. The process is much more enjoyable than the typical (fix-it via the flavor-of-the-month engagement) intervention. Many people will enjoy contributing to the employee engagement process—and success.

Communication Excellence

An executive coach will endeavor to ensure that every step a

CEO takes, in terms of communication, is successful. The executive coach understands how every communication has a ripple effect throughout the organization. Any communication missteps will slow down the improvement process. By working together to improve communication, the coach and CEO will move the firm forward. Obviously, nothing is sure proof, but many things can be done to minimize risk.

A personal example from my teaching experience: One of the most successful courses I created was called "Branding." Roughly 50 percent of the course was branding, and 50 percent was pricing. Obviously if the goal were to develop a high-end brand, choosing a low price would not be an appropriate fit. One rather entertaining aspect of the course involved viewing how organizations explain price changes (an important part of corporate communication). Frankly, most organizations do a terrible job in this regard. Most pricing communication is impersonal (as if a company forgets how the customer feels about the changes). Typically such communication focuses on the problems facing the company rather than on problems customers will face. For example, companies often didn't allow enough time for customers to adjust to a price change, that is, the price change was instantaneous. Also, price changes didn't allow a purchasing organization (possibly a wholesaler or retailer) to adjust budgets and make propitious inventory changes before a proposed price change. What makes the pricing process less than efficient is marginal reasoning used to explain the pricing decision and clumsy implementation of price changes.

Bad communication delivered by the CEO means she will die the death of a thousand qualifications in an attempt to explain it. Recently the CEO of United proved the point in dealing with the incident involving a doctor being dragged off of a plane in Chicago. All outcomes of a potential communication need to be carefully evaluated. Input from those outside the organization is helpful in understanding how a message will be received.

Poor communication often encourages talented, articulate leaders to opt for organizations that appear to be more professional. CEOs and top managers are measured most clearly in two ways: (1) by their oral and written communication skills and (2) by their ability to acquire and retain talented employees. Turnover among hourly people is troublesome, but turnover of leaders is both demoralizing and expensive.

Public Speaking

Coaches assist with communication and normally are not satisfied unless improvement takes place. It was no secret that George W. Bush was not a good speaker, and remarkably he didn't improve much during his eight years as president. Barack Obama was viewed as a better communicator—because he usually read off a teleprompter. Neither of these presidents was particularly effective at speaking impromptu. My best advice for both would have been to stay on the teleprompter—and hire a coach to perfect the art of speaking when off script.

Note that one doesn't have to be a great speaker to coach speakers. The best communication coach I ever had, who worked with me while I was a member of the National Speakers Association, was not good speaker himself. Improvement comes by learning to let others help improve communication. It starts by admitting problems exist.

CEOs rarely ask for input on their speaking or writing, but most need help. Even the tone of a speech can have a dramatic impact. For example, a serious tone is helpful if the organization is facing a significant challenge such a budgetary problem. In similar fashion, there are times when a fun-loving tone is more appropriate.

For example, during corporate get-togethers, there are normally several speeches delivered by various presenters. Individually or as a group, presenters too often send mixed signals. Maybe an executive employs her comical sense of humor, but if the meeting is a bit too serious for this speech, the message will not be well received. An excellent coach can train each speaker and will often help write the speeches. Creating a common theme and common tone limits the mixed messages.

An executive must not rest on a false self-perception that he or she is an excellent communicator. Unfortunately an insider often will avoid helping a CEO with communication issues, because such input is not politically expedient. The coach understands that communication is paramount, because it ultimately impacts the entire organization.

Personalized Communication

Communication, almost without exception, reveals the CEO's true heart. Quick example: What is the most powerful communication a CEO can provide? The answer is the handwritten note. Not an email, which is often an electronic form letter. One corporate president told a story about a canned form letter he received. The computer accidently addressed it to President XYZ at ——— Corporation. Seeing the "off-beat" nature of the correspondence, he read it aloud to his key leadership team. It went something like this: "Dear President XYZ, thank you for your interest in our firm's products. Our goal is to pursue excellence and build it into everything we do. We have great respect for the similar path you have followed, President XYZ. Believe us, President XYZ, we will provide the tremendous service you are accustomed to . . ." You get the idea, most of us were laughing so hard we were crying.

Now for a positive example: I once had a client who highly respected Dr. John Maxwell. A few years earlier, Dr. Maxwell and I had worked on a project together, and we became friends. Not a shock—John is a people person. I knew my client enjoyed many of John's books; I asked if John would write my client a handwritten note. John did so, on a piece of beautifully embossed paper. As you might imagine, the note is framed and hanging on the wall in my client's office. Do you think an email can compete with something like this? Not likely.

Finally, the handwritten note represents raw power. It is extremely personal and should not be written to praise in a general, but rather in a specific, way. Such a message can lead to some amazing motivation. Occasionally what is said is so helpful that a person has it rolling in the conscious mind for the rest of his or her life. CEOs should maximum the power of this tool. It also sends a powerful "cultural" message since many colleagues will get wind of this note. In summary, a handwritten note to thank an employee for a job well done is incredibly powerful!

A Matter of Perspective

A coach will challenge the CEO to change his or her perspective about communication. Change the heart, and you change the communication. Warmth can be taught (take one step at a time), and major improvements in communication logically follow. Engineering and technology CEOs often struggle with the "warmth" issue, but such limitations can be addressed if the CEO is willing.

Chapter 9

Empowering Your People

Great organizations help people to explore and to experience satisfaction in their work. Google, Apple, Facebook, and many of the emerging fast-growth, technology start-ups boast about open environments, flexible hours, teamwork, knowledge development, fun at work, rest breaks, and the opportunity to travel.

They encourage people to follow their natural talents, to explore and thereby experience satisfaction in their work. People in entrepreneurial start-ups are initially forced to do a variety of functions. Eventually CEOs will want to hire to fill in talent gaps. Sometimes they find it expedient to outsource to other organizations that deliver certain functional results more efficiently. With employees fully engaged, what often surfaces? Powerful, compelling, creative, and profitable organizations driven by talented people using their strengths.

Is it possible for all companies to enjoy talent-oriented workplaces? Absolutely. Technology companies have an advantage in that they must lean into the legitimate talents (often demonstrated) of those they are hiring. In these companies, required skills and talent are easy to see; if they are missing, changes must be made. With assessments and simple intervention techniques, any organization can sharpen its application of talent.

Many have learned to focus on managing employees whom the late Peter Drucker termed "knowledge workers." Different from employing physical labor or managing production, managing "knowledge" requires freeing up higher-level thinking skills and allowing room for freedom and exploration. Teams seem to be the best answer. When teams work well, people feel valued. A successful CEO must create an organization that allows for employee engagement and consequently for people to live out their work lives by using their legitimate talents and strengths. In a competitive marketplace, a company must have a clear focus on developing talent. Otherwise the finest people will leave to find greener pastures.

Empowerment Recap

We've previously discussed the value of flattening organizations, reducing levels of middle management. When an organization is flattened, a CEO immediately realizes the strengths of her or his people. One quickly recognizes people who do—and don't—have the confidence to achieve great things. Information helps build confidence, but engagement is the key to building confidence. Focusing on talent can breed confidence, and confidence normally breeds success.

Arthur Ashe reportedly said, "One important key to success is self-confidence. An important key to self-confidence is preparation." It is difficult to gain confidence if one is constantly controlled by the powers that be. It makes more sense to let employees work to figure it out, and to let them enjoy the confidence gained when they have success. In a lean organization, a leader works to push the decision-making down the organizational structure.

Empowerment has become a significant method used to create flexibility within the larger organizations. Empowerment is primarily a structure and process that allows employees to take an active role in decision-making within their organization.

As I have worked in various organizations, I have seen empowerment from a variety of perspectives. Historically empowerment was based on humanistic principles such as self-direction, autonomy, radical individualism, and so on. Empowerment now works best in organizations that knowingly or unknowingly focus on the simple concept of right and wrong—organizations with a foundational value system that respects individuals and the value they contribute to the team.

In an empowered organization, the power flows both to the top and to the bottom of the organizational chart. Leaders in the middle will lose power and often their traditional positions. Fortunately, by the time the empowerment process is in place, these leaders are often given opportunities to lead project teams, sometimes ending up with better positions than they started with. Many end up being viewed as true leaders in the organization.

As the layers of management are removed, the empowered organization moves to a horizontal, process orientation; CEOs must be able to view managers in a new way. Sounds easy, but it is not. Here a coach can prove helpful. Example: think of someone you have had issues with because you felt that person was not serious about his responsibilities. This person has not performed well on the job. But . . . this person may be very successful in an empowered organization where he can work based on personal talents and strengths. A CEO must have an open mind, looking for positive appreciation as this person with recast responsibilities learns to successfully operate in an empowered organization.

Changing One's View

When people follow their hearts, positive changes can be quite dramatic. My son went off to college in California (seven states away). Josh was young, immature, not very articulate, and not especially wise about how to work within authority frameworks. After four years of college, his earrings were out; his communication skills were polished; he graduated top of his class and was consequently awarded a free Millennial MBA. After the graduation ceremony, Josh presented personalized coffee mugs to all of his adult mentors. On each cup, he had a picture of the mentor and himself. He included— printed on the cup—some personal thoughts about what each man meant to him. As Josh presented the gifts, he had these men in tears. He was so articulate and so polished, I wondered, what did you do with my son? Well, he had time to build some of his talents into true strengths, and in the process he gained confidence. As a result, I had to think in new ways about Josh—as you might well change your views of employees, once languishing but now thriving.

Once you recalibrate for strengths and flatten the organization, workers will likely also change their views of top management's expertise as well as limitations—limitations that may actually diminish as subordinates take on more responsibility. The responsibility that used to rest on top management is gone. Employees often feel quite different when they must "own" some of the responsibility.

Based on personal experience, I can tell you that one is never sure which managers will survive and prosper in the newly empowered organization. Each employee is now given the opportunity to demonstrate his or her talent. A CEO who can stand back and view his or her managers in a new way must be very secure and gracious indeed. It is more about creating an engaging work environment than it is about pounding employees into submission.

Enhancing Employee Communications

In rapidly growing companies, little or no downsizing will be needed. A firm positioned for growth will make sure that talent is refocused on new opportunities. There is no better way to prepare for growth than to get employees engaged in their jobs.

Unfortunately top-down structures do not create clear communication. As you move from the bottom to the top of the organization, the communications become slightly distorted at each level of management. Normally this is not a result of blatant dishonesty; people just naturally distort the information to protect people above or below them.

As noted earlier, empowerment pushes power to the bottom and to the top of the organization, because subordinates communicate with their top managers face to face. Accountability is enhanced, and excuses for nonperformance simply won't fly. There is no way to pass responsibility to someone else, no way to shift blame.

At first, until trust is developed, communication about strengths and limitations can be painful, difficult to digest.

Reconsidering Credentials

Empowered organizations work best when they do not create artificial barriers for people, such as "everyone must have a college education" or "everyone needs to have three years of electrical engineering experience." Responsible CEOs understand that performance is more important than credentials. (Have you ever wondered why organizations want applicants to have three to four years of experience? They are saying, "practice on someone else." The assumption is that prospective employees are likely to know what they are good at and what they enjoy based on previous experiences; it may even be noticeable on their résumé in terms of past accomplishments. This is not the most efficient way to determine talent.)

Interestingly, studies consistently indicate that entrepreneurs are not typically college educated. Why is this so? At the university, young people are taught to follow processes, plans, and rules. Business professors will say, how can you start a business without a business plan? Rules just seem to rule.

One of my favorite Warren Bennis quotes is "Straight 'A' students never seem to get over it" (*On Becoming a Leader*). They want to know exactly what it takes to get an A. Unfortunately the real world does not work that way. You have to go with the flow and be creative.

I'm not arguing for the elimination of hiring criteria but rather making the case for more relevant engagement-oriented, selection processes. Every person has strengths and limitations. Every person has God-given talents and abilities. Every person has a personality temperament that kicks in and affects situational reactions. A human resources department's job is to clarify talent, strengths, temperament, attitude, skills, and values.

Understanding these personal variables coupled with discernment about character qualities allows a CEO to have a better opportunity of determining potential success than by using the aforementioned artificial barriers created by a top-down structure.

As leaders take their people through an empowerment process, they will see the best and the worst in their people. The process is career threatening to people who have spent years working their way up the corporate ladder. Fear is always the first response to change. As the old power structure begins to crumble and the new emerges, a coach may spend many hours talking leaders through the changes.

I remember talking to an organization's vice

president about how it felt to have three thousand employees working for him one day and then find himself working for three thousand employees the next day. A new form of leadership was emerging, and he was positioned to serve the field reps, those closest to the customer. In reality, he shifted from vice president of operations to a position of trainer, teacher, encourager, business plan evaluator, internal consultant, enabler, and financier. He was a top leader, but his job and his methods were radically altered.

Envisioning Survival, then Greatness

Leaders must be confident that implementing an empowering paradigm shift is right and crucial to the survival of the organization. They will need an enormous amount of patience and wisdom, because employees will be watching their every move. What they do and how they do it will speak volumes. Empowerment thus becomes a defining moment for leaders who performed well in the old "top-down" organization. Many survive and prosper, and many will move on.

Perhaps the most telling component of the empowerment process will be the vision that drives it. The most basic question every human asks in life is "why?" During the empowerment process, expect to hear the *why* question asked on a regular basis. I believe some why questions are self-serving, such as, why do I need to change the way I do things? I like to answer such questions by asking, are you doing these things primarily for yourself or because they are in the best interests of the organization and the customers we serve?

I believe more legitimate questions involve larger issues, such as, why do we need to grow so fast? It's essential for a CEO to learn the difference between self-serving questions and those that deserve a listening ear.

Survival is a powerful motivator. The top-down structure is too expensive, too clumsy, and too inefficient. Proactive companies do not wait until they are in trouble. They are both future oriented and growth oriented. Growth is considered a stewardship issue. If companies are dealing with obsolete products, growth may not even be an option in the short-run.

Modern economies do not offer much forgiveness for companies that only want to play defense. If a high school team takes on the Indiana University basketball team, and they get IU to agree to play only defense, sooner or later a high school player will make a basket and win the game. Defense and neutrality don't work in our dynamic worldwide economy. The leveling process and price transparency driven by the Internet means safe harbors no longer exist.

Technology companies have to institutionalize the process of change to survive. Creative destruction is the norm for such companies. They must destroy today's winning products to quickly advance the products of tomorrow. My past students never seemed to understand why they got an IPod with a new Mac. The perk was primarily a way to get rid of outdated products. Employees need to constantly think about what products and services should come next. How can they better serve their customers and find underserved market segments? Think innovation!

Service companies have no excuse when it comes to "growth," since they can change a service by simply changing their mind-set. There is cost in changing services but nothing compared to the cost of dealing with obsolete products. Service companies stop growing because of antiquated systems and ideas. These can ultimately be changed if CEOs have the will to do so.

How we define accomplishment can be a problem. I think vision is essential, but just hearing about how much money a founding family or corporation wants to make is not a vision that will motivate an employee. Do not expect people to buy "empowerment" simply because some CEO desires a bigger profit. This type of vision doesn't make people jump out of the bed in the morning. Empowerment breaks down barriers and makes opportunity available to nearly everyone.

We mentioned values in a previous chapter, but here I touch on it again briefly in terms of vision: CEOs should provide employees freedom without compromising their values. CEOs do not empower people to create their own corporate culture. Rather, they help their people to accept positive corporate values and then provide the freedom within the culture that allows for positive performance. The Golden Rule does not allow the employees' values to drive the organization. The shared organizational values drive the empowered company.

Wrap-Up

I want to tie all of this together with some cautions. First, remember that there often is intensely negative thinking by employees when an organization goes through an empowerment process. People love to be empowered, but they do not enjoy empowering those below them. Lord Acton was correct: "power tends to corrupt, and absolute power corrupts absolutely," so those in power don't relish handing it to subordinates.

Second, if you decide to empower your people, be blatantly honest all the way through the change process. You may have some problems as a result of your honesty but, in the end, taking the moral high road can pay huge dividends.

As a coach, I tell CEOs that I will not be dishonest nor will I hedge when people ask questions. If well planned, there will be minimal damage by telling the truth; one gains credibility that is priceless. Some people won't like the change and will self-select to change jobs.

Third, do not expect a smooth road. Change involves significant pain. People go through the adjustment process at different speeds. First, they must achieve an intellectual acceptance of what has changed and later a heart acceptance.

Finally, you will have to help people get out of the huddle and back into the game. People will stay in suspended animation as long as you allow them to. Expect to be surprised by both good and bad things along the way. Some people will run with empowerment. Some will work counter to your proposals. Whenever you lead, someone will be throwing rocks from the cheap seats. Be sure of the moral rightness of what you are doing; it makes all the difference.

To guide the process, create a steering committee, composed of employees from different levels and functions of the company committed to empowerment. Members of the steering committee can help identify and resolve potential and real issues. Steering committee members should be people who are trusted by the vast majority of employees.

Leadership is often a lonely road, so do not expect encouragement along the way. I have noticed that during tough times I am hampered by my own inattention to my personal and professional growth. You have to pull off-site occasionally and find a way to refresh your spirit, or you may be unable to stay the course.

Do not try to do this by yourself. Consider having some business mentors who have lived through empowerment restructuring. This should be a partner who is not in the organization you are leading. Don't be afraid to implement empowerment. But remember, if it were easy, everyone would be doing it. Engagement will be a result of empowerment, and the results will be remarkable.

Corporate Culture—Engagement Helps Convert "Order-Takers" into "Owners"

Remove negative mind-sets to create a positive motivational environment.

1. Internal marketing. What can you do to get your employees on the same page? Whether you lead a for-profit or nonprofit, customers are the ultimate rallying point. Problems do not go away. Openly admit past sins. Ask for forgiveness and move on. The resulting "changed behavior " Can lead to positive actions by others.

2. Encourage everyone to have both a personal and a corporate vision. Help employees achieve their personal vision while they help to achieve the corporate vision. Make sure all are on the same page and motivated.

3. Incentives, incentives, incentives—understand the pluses and minuses of incentives. Incentives have to be easy to understand. Complexity can complicate incentives, and unclear incentives won't lead to motivation. Choose goals that are "worthy."

4. To build teams, break down social classes and cliques within the organization. Be sure to show appreciation for everyone. Make sure your people have time together both at and after work. Create a compelling place to work. Know the personal values of the various generations that work with you.

5. Choose your corporate heroes wisely. Change traditions that are not positive. Think about building a fast-track system for your future leaders.

Your Job Is to Help Find Ways for Your People to Advance....

- Create career paths.
- Train to advance.
- Support your dreamers.
- Provide space to try things out.
- The only stupid idea is the one that doesn't get shared.

Chapter 10

Where Coaching and Consulting Converge

Leaders are expected to lead. The coach should not make strategic decisions but rather guide and support the leader's growth. An effective leader must both develop and implement effective strategies. Strategy involves choosing the future versus settling for the status quo. As established earlier, executive coaches don't make line decisions. The purpose is simply to help leaders grow. The model below indicates what external environments the leader should evaluate.

An executive coach can facilitate the growth of the leader to broaden a perspective. Let's start with a narrow view and consider ever-broadening perspectives.

Capabilities that need to be acquired

Accessible cross-industry knowledge

Industry wisdom

Company knowledge

First, strategic decisions could be based on the current knowledge, that which is being employed and hidden capabilities lying dormant within the firm. StrengthsFinder and coaching will accomplish much of what a hunting dog accomplishes. The CEO has the gun, but the coach helps to flush out hidden talent, go after the prey (reel them in), and help retrieve those talents.

Second, strategic decisions might be based on talents of employees that are currently (one hopes) being developed into strengths. If you were helping an executive develop his strategic talent, you would be pushing him to get involved in a variety of educational experiences. For example, executive education programs at reputable universities would be a wonderful place to start. What perfect timing to develop a strategic strength

Third, strategic decisions could consider current industry wisdom. This is normally known as a follower strategy. Question: why is your company not the industry leader? By leader, I'm not referring to size but rather having the best competitive advantage, the most compelling innovations, in other words, the new ideas that could potentially transform the entire industry. Therefore, step 1 might involve becoming a respected innovator in your industry before you try to determine the game-changing innovations that will have an impact far beyond your industry.

Fourth, an even broader perspective can be gained by cross-industry ideas. Ideas that are currently beyond the mind-set of industry leaders can break down the established rules for how things are done. One very small example proves the point.

Early in my career, I was a marketing leader for commercial builder. When selling large projects, a common tool to secure the sale was referred to as a "letter of intent"—

given by the potential purchaser to the contractor who would be hired in the not-to-distant future to build the commercial building. Seems backward, especially since the contractor will likely be the one who creates the actual document. Stay with me. What we are striving for is commitment. What about taking the construction-industry's "letter of intent" model and using it to facilitate a coaching agreement?

Note this example of the letter of intent that might be used for my business:

Letter of Intent

Date _____
From: **FF, Jr.**

      CEO of XYZ

To: Dr. Phil Millage, President
          Inspire Executive Coaching, LLC
          Fishers, IN 46038

Dear Phil,

It is our intention to use your services for a development program with our executive team.

Although this is not a legally binding agreement, we are making this commitment so you can continue the planning process. We will look forward to working with you based on the planning we have done with you thus far.

Sincerely,

FF, Jr.
CEO of XYZ

Obviously, a coach would not do this until a relationship was in place and it appeared that the plan was coming together. You as the coach are testing for commitment. What this letter accomplishes is that it puts a halt to the buying (request for proposal) process. Basically, FF is agreeing to work with Dr. Phil so he discontinues talking with other vendors. FF will feel positive about it partially because he now knows what he wants and thus isn't interested in continuing a dialogue with multiple parties. More than 90 percent of the time, a purchaser will follow through once he has put his name on the line. Now you might think, Phil that is pretty pushy! But if I cannot test the commitment level, I may be making proposals forever and never truly get the job. FF might be harvesting my best ideas to work with a vendor who has less to offer but can do so at a better price. If FF won't sign, he isn't committed, and it would be wise for me to refocus on a prospective client who is committed.

So my cross-industry idea was to use a letter of intent for a new, substantial nursing home project. We implemented a variety of marketing tools, such as providing "under the roof banquets" when the facility was barely under the roof. The naysayers on the nursing home leadership team said such an agreement could not be used in a medical model. I found no legal issues. I successfully sold them on the idea, and we had the facility occupied in a fraction of the normal time, saving my client millions of dollars. The idea came from a different industry, but we made a simple application to a new industry. The coach could have the CEO look at other industries to see what he or she can discover and potentially apply.

Fifth, often unique leadership capabilities must be acquired. If you've never taken a product nationwide, you might consider bringing someone on board who has done so in the past. The Shark Tank program allows innovators/inventors who create new products to sell their ideas to would-be investors. Often inventors and innovators have no idea how to take a breakthrough product to the marketplace. The rule of thumb in marketing is that 50 percent of your cost will be marketing cost. The bottom-line is . . . you might need Lori Greiner from QVC to develop an online shopping venue that could be used from anywhere. You won't have time to reinvent the wheel. Learn to appreciate what others can bring to the table.

Sixth, if innovation and inventions become central to your business, you could quickly be in the business of changing many of the rules (how things are done) across many industries. Thomas Edison's inventions have touched nearly every modern industry. In publishing, Malcolm Gladwell is impacting many industries. Larry Page and Sergey Brin, having set the foundation for Google, changed everything. Very rarely does one person change the world. It will more likely require an amazing team to do that.

One of my students from a few years back was and is an amazing entrepreneur. He is the only student I told, "Forget about working for someone else; you will hate it." As he began developing his technology business, he realized he needed a skilled marketer and a skilled technologist. Small problem. The people he needed to bring on were already making a significant income in their careers. As I coached this young man, he had to come to terms with the facts. One fact was that he would have to live on a fraction of what he would need to pay his partners, even though he was the CEO. His company is now a fast-growing business-to-business technology firm, and they have already purchased a complementary company that can allow them to create some "off-the-shelf" products of their own.

What made this work? He was young, brilliant, a natural salesman with phenomenal people skills; he had an amazing work ethic, but, more important, he had zero hard-and-fast rules about how things had to work. He quickly created a powerful team, included a strong values-driven internal environment, and developed a fun place to work where other young, talented tech types would love to come on board.

Paradigms and Patterns

If you are unable to change, I recommend that you not hire a coach, because the executive coach will want you to participate in new learning and new experiences that will quickly make your old patterns appear irrelevant. Sure, you will make more money, have more fun, and enjoy the satisfaction of what you accomplish, but you will have to go through the challenge of breaking the rules and dealing with the patterns that got you to where you are now—both good and bad patterns.

Negative patterns, some which are predictable, can be improved with the help of a coach. One example could be the inability of an insecure CEO to take input. Let's face it, the insider will never be convincing enough to help the CEO change. Consequently, if people stop providing suggestions, you might need to get ready for some unpleasant surprises. The flip side is the CEO who faces a constant barrage unwarranted opinions, many of which are a waste of time. The coach will help the CEO create ground rules for how much and what type of input is helpful. Once decisions are made, implementation of new products, services, and processes will need to take place in a rather dictatorial fashion. Second-guessing your way through an implementation process is a sure path to failure.

An executive coach will be interested in what is both predictable and unpredictable about a CEO's actions. The idea is to build on the positives and minimize the negatives. Occasionally teaching the CEO how to be more or less predictable (given certain situations) can be facilitated by a coach. A couple of examples can prove the point. Let's say a CEO is predictably close minded, that is, she comes to committee meetings with her mind made up. Another might be open minded until a decision is made, and then the decision is never altered even if it is disastrous. A third CEO is predictably budget minded even when small adjustments would send a powerful message that people matter. Different situations call for different styles of decision-making. The CEO and coach will collaborate to think through how to improve decision-making patterns.

A CEO might be most influenced by the last person he had lunch with. Such a leader might wonder why everyone wants to have lunch before the final strategic planning session. Every leader has patterns. The coach wants to help the CEO discover and ultimately understand managerial patterns and help the CEO reform some while building up others.

Chapter 11

Coaching CEOs Creates Results

The coach's desire is that his or her helpful input and educational prodding would lead the CEO to acknowledge a need for and welcome personal and professional change. Subsequently the coach and CEO collaborate to build an incremental process for growth. It is impossible for the CEO to change everything at once. So coaching involves providing new knowledge, new methods, and ideas with the goal of positive change. The coaching process is incremental and measurable. Mutually agreed goals guide the coaching process.

In a perfect world, the coach will be hired because the CEO is highly motivated to improve performance. If the CEO has been pressured to hire the coach, the CEO's reluctance may impede progress. A good coach will work to partner with the CEO and to demonstrate how this collaborative process can lead to organizational and career success. If there is no desire to grow, the process becomes nearly impossible. Don't waste your money!

The entire process should be collaborative rather than adversarial. Conflict will be part of the process, but healthy conflict is the goal. Conflict can be a catalyst for change. The coach's goal is to facilitate substantial improvement across a variety of fronts.

In summary, the coach is focused on helping the

CEO develop personal talents into legitimate strengths. For example, if the CEO has the gift of communication, specifically, a talent for speaking, the coach will want to facilitate the development of that talent. Excellence is the goal, and excellence should be recognizable to the entire organization.

The coach understands that leadership from the middle doesn't work—that the coaching process begins with the CEO. The dividend is when the CEO witnesses the larger organization positively changing as a result of the improvements in his or her performance. The coach and CEO share one important goal. Both desire organizational success and enhanced profitability. Isn't that what your job is about? It's time to make your move.

Significant Roles for Coaching in Your Organization

- Talent hunters—finding talent usually involves a collaborative process. One more set of eyes helps to make excellent decisions.
- Talent repositioning—assessing talent provides an opportunity to retool without changing personnel.
- Talent developers—this was a responsibility that Peter Drucker said rests with leadership.
- Talent harvesters—once one has the right people in the right place, goals are set, people get to work, and soon the organization is harvesting the positive results.
- Conflict resolution—one can have the right person in the right place, and yet conflict still has to be dealt with for the organization to excel.

- Communication enhancers—many top managers need help with creating positive, effective communication.
- Decision-making skills—healthy conflict often emerges when there are differences in talent. This kind of conflict if well channeled can lead to superior decisions.
- Strategy and planning—involves coaching about methods for securing the right leaders coupled with preparing the culture for change. Coaches can be true collaborators.
- Emotional intelligence—involves appropriately using interpersonal skills, empathy, and listening skills. As an example, "likability" continues to be an important quality needed by CEOs.
- Motivation—motivation grows and feeds on enhanced employee engagement.
- Coaching—ensures that mentoring and people development is everywhere at work in the organization. Computers lead to enhancements in productivity, but effective leadership is even more critical.
- Team building—nothing can stop a totally turned on team.
- Training—marginal skills lead to less than remarkable results.

Empowerment and shared leadership—letting people use their strengths is intrinsically motivational. Learn to let go of the tendency to employ misapplied talent.

About the Author

Dr. Phil Millage has a lifetime of consulting and coaching experience working with seasoned and emerging leaders in more than a hundred organizations. This multiple-industry experience has allowed Dr. Millage to witness amazing breakthroughs in one industry and subsequently to apply those innovations in a new industry. Breaking the prevailing paradigm is always the goal.

Phil's expertise is most valued where the impact is potentially the greatest—with CEOs, senior managers, and board members. He has witnessed firsthand that as CEOs grow and develop their organizations naturally follow suit.

Dr. Millage spent the formative part of his career in sales and marketing, followed by professional speaking and consulting, then on to the development of his companies, and finally to coaching CEOs. This synthesis of experience and learning provided Dr. Millage a uniquely inspiring perspective.

The most common comments from CEOs note Dr. Millage's ability to recognize talent in others and his strong desire to help develop it. He is known first and foremost as an advocate and developer of CEOs and secondly as an idea-oriented, strategic thinker/paradigm breaker.

Dr. Millage has been privileged to teach at four excellent universities, across several business disciplines, and to participate in student/faculty research at Oxford, Cambridge, and Harvard.

For a professional _speaking_ engagement or _coaching_,

you may contact Phil Millage

www.inspireexecutivecoaching.com

phil@inspireexecutivecoaching.com

or directly at philmillage@me.com